Militant
Modernism

Militant
Modernism

Owen Hatherley

BOOKS

Winchester, UK
Washington, USA

First published by O Books, 2008
O Books is an imprint of John Hunt Publishing Ltd., The Bothy, Deershot Lodge, Park Lane, Ropley,
Hants, SO24 0BE, UK
office1@o-books.net
www.o-books.net

Distribution in:	South Africa
	Alternative Books
UK and Europe	altbook@peterhyde.co.za
Orca Book Services	Tel: 021 555 4027 Fax: 021 447 1430
orders@orcabookservices.co.uk	
Tel: 01202 665432 Fax: 01202 666219	Text copyright Owen Hatherley 2008
Int. code (44)	
	Design: Stuart Davies
USA and Canada	
NBN	ISBN: 978 1 84694 176 4
custserv@nbnbooks.com	
Tel: 1 800 462 6420 Fax: 1 800 338 4550	All rights reserved. Except for brief quotations
	in critical articles or reviews, no part of this
Australia and New Zealand	book may be reproduced in any manner without
Brumby Books	prior written permission from the publishers.
sales@brumbybooks.com.au	
Tel: 61 3 9761 5535 Fax: 61 3 9761 7095	The rights of Owen Hatherley as author have
	been asserted in accordance with the
Far East (offices in Singapore, Thailand,	Copyright, Designs and Patents Act 1988.
Hong Kong, Taiwan)	
Pansing Distribution Pte Ltd	
kemal@pansing.com	A CIP catalogue record for this book is available
Tel: 65 6319 9939 Fax: 65 6462 5761	from the British Library.

Printed by CPI Antony Rowe, Chippenham, Wiltshire

O Books operates a distinctive and ethical publishing philosophy in
all areas of its business, from its global network of authors to
production and worldwide distribution.
This book is produced on FSC certified stock, within ISO14001
standards. The printer plants sufficient trees each year through
the Woodland Trust to absorb the level of emitted carbon in
its production.

CONTENTS

Forwards (not Forgetting)   3
Retracing/Eldorado for the Working Class

The Brutishness of British Modernism   15
An Englishman's Home is his Fortress/The Aesthetics of Hell/'The Great London Vortex': Wyndham Lewis as Chav/The Greater London Council Vortex: A Bit of the Old Ultraviolence/Everyone on Park Hill Came in Unison at 4.13 AM/Future Ruins

A Hole into the Future   43
Red Planet Mars/Theories of Ruin Value/The Revolution of Everyday Life/The Institute for the Transformation of Mankind

Revolutionary Orgasm Problems   70
Energetic Functionalism/Physical Culture in the Love Hotel and the Minimum Dwelling/Make Way for Winged Eros!/From Sexpol to Sexploitation/I Still Dream of Orgonon

Alienation Affects   97
Godot Vs Galileo/Who's Afraid of the Verfremdungseffekt?/A Threepenny Film and a Threepenny Lawsuit/A Short Course in Realism from the Perspective of the Police/The Half That's Never Been Told

Afterwards   119
The Unmaking of a Counter-Culture/Towards a New Proletcult

Acknowledgements   127

Notes   128

LIST OF IMAGES

Forwards

0.1: Weston Shore, Southampton, designed by L. Berger for Southampton City Council (1967). Photograph by the author, 2007

0.2: Wyndham Court, Southampton, designed by Lyons Israel Ellis for Southampton City Council (1969). Photograph by the author, 2007

0.3: Tecton (Skinner, Bailey and Lubetkin), Bevin Court (1951). Photograph by Joel Anderson, 2007

Part 1

1.1: Barrier Point, Silvertown, London, designed for Barratt Homes by Goddard Manton (2000). Photograph by Joel Anderson, 2008

1.2: Spiller's Millennium Mills, Silvertown, London (1933). Photograph by Joel Anderson, 2008

1.3 D Silo, Pontoon Dock, London (1920). Photograph by Joel Anderson, 2008.

1.4: Edward Wadsworth, 'Drydocked for Scaling and Painting', on cover of the school textbook *Transport Design*, by Corin Hughes-Stanton (from the collection of the author)

1.5: Robin Hood Gardens, Poplar, London. Designed by Alison and Peter Smithson (1972). Photograph by the author, 2005

1.6: Thamesmead, designed by the Greater London Council Architects Dept (1967-71). Photograph by the author, 2005

1.7: Prospective drawings of Thamesmead, 1967 (from the collection of the author)

1.8: Barbican Estate, London, designed by Chamberlin Powell and Bon (1958-82). Photograph by Douglas Murphy, 2008

1.9: Eros House, Catford, London, designed by Owen Luder Partnership (1962). Photograph by Joel Anderson, 2008

1.10 and 1.11, Ferrier Estate, Kidbrooke, Greater London Council Architects Dept (1968-72). Photographs by Joel Anderson, 2008

Part 2

2.1: Still from Yakov Protazanov's *Aelita* (1924)

2.2 N.P Prusakov & G.I Borisov, *Travel to Mars* (1926)

2.3 Richard Pare, photograph of the Palace of the Press, Baku, designed by Semen Pen (1932)

2.4 Richard Pare, photograph of Shaumian Workers Club, Baku, designed by Leonid Vesnin (1929)

2.5 Richard Pare, photograph of the Vasilievsky Factory Kitchen, Leningrad, designed by Baruchev, Gilter, Meerzon and Rubachik (1930-31)

2.6 Richard Pare, photograph of the Narvskaya Factory Kitchen, Leningrad, designed by Baruchev, Gilter, Meerzon and Rubachik (1928-31)

2.7 Svoboda Workers' Club, Moscow, designed by Konstantin Melnikov, 1927. Photograph by Nikolai Onoufriev.

2.8 Gustav Klutsis, 'To live culturally is to work productively' (1932)

2.9 and 2.10 Stills from Sergei Eisenstein's *The General Line* (1929): Gosprom in Kharkov and the Collective Farm by Andrei Burov.

Part 3

3.1 'Love Operation', by Lydia Thompson, 2007

3.2 Still from Abram Room's *Bed and Sofa* (1927)

3.3 Narkomfin Building, Moscow, designed by Moisei Ginzburg and Ignati Milinis, 1929. Photograph by Nikolai Onoufriev.

3.4 G.M Shegal, 'Down with Kitchen Slavery!' (1933)

3.5, 3.6, Stills from Makavejev's *The Switchboard Operator* (1967)

3.7, 3.8. 3.9, Stills from Makavejev's *WR – Mysteries of the Organism* (1970)

Part 4

4.1 and 4.2 Stills from G.W Pabst, *The Threepenny Opera* (1930)

4.3, 4.4, 4.5, 4.6 Stills from Slatan Dudow, *Kuhle Wampe, oder Wem Gehort Die Welt?* (1932)

Afterwards

5.1, 'Slumber Lions', Lydia Thompson, 2007

5.2 Eros House, Catford, photograph by Joel Anderson, 2008

'Practical people have a way of saying 'that has been tried, and failed.' Why, of course it failed. Do you suppose everybody ever played off a piece of Right on the eternal piano without striking false notes at first? Failed! – yes, and it will fail fifty times over, depend on it, as long as your fingers are baby's fingers; your business is not to mind your fingers, but to look at the written notes.

When people first try to walk with an Alpine pole, they always use it the wrong way, You show them the right way, which upon proceeding to practice, they as a matter of course, immediately get a very awkward fall, and get up rubbing their shins. If they were 'practical' people, they would immediately say in a grave manner 'That has been tried, and failed.' But most Alpine prospective walkers having some poetry in them, they say in an unpractical manner 'Well, we'll try again', and thus 'walking by faith', after a few more tumbles, come to be able to cross a glacier.'

John Ruskin, 'A Defence of the Idealists' (1853)[1]

This book is dedicated to the Southampton City Council Architects Department.

Forwards (not Forgetting)

Retracing

Erase the Traces. Destroy, in order to create. Build a new world on the ruins of the old. This, it is often thought, is the Modernist imperative, but what of it if the new society never emerged? We have been cheated out of the future, yet the future's ruins lie about us, hidden or ostentatiously rotting. So what would it mean, then, to look for the future's remnants? To uncover clues about those who wanted, as Walter Benjamin put it, to 'live without traces'? Can we, should we, try and excavate utopia?

To do so might be a final, bitter betrayal of Modernism itself. Although there have always been several strains in Modernism, one of the most dominant has always been based on the demand, made by Bertolt Brecht in his 1926 *Handbook for City Dwellers* to *'erase the traces!'* Benjamin's gloss on this refrain is in a fragmentary 1933 piece, 'Short Shadows'. Straightforwardly, what Benjamin wanted to 'erase' was the stifling pile-up of historicist detritus that made up the bourgeois aesthetic. Benjamin writes of

Weston Shore, Southampton

3

their interiors that 'living in these plush apartments was nothing more than leaving traces made by habits. Even the rage expressed when the least little thing broke was perhaps merely the reaction of a person who felt that someone had obliterated 'the traces of his days on earth'. The traces he had left on cushions and armchairs, that his relatives had left in photos, and that his possessions had left in linings and etuis and that sometimes made these rooms look as overcrowded as halls full of funerary urns.'[2] But this is exactly what Modernism sets out to ruthlessly rub out: 'the new architects, with their glass and steel (have) created rooms in which it is hard to leave traces.'

In 'Experience and Poverty' later in that terrible year, Benjamin cites the Bauhaus, Le Corbusier and Adolf Loos, all now exemplars of what tends to be called the 'heroic age' of modern architecture, as exemplary architects of erasing traces, and expresses the hope that their new world will survive its enemies. We find the traces effaced again, with added drama, in his portrait of a man who has internalised Modernism into the fibre of his being: 'The Destructive Character knows only one watchword: make room. And only one activity: clearing away. His need for fresh air and open space is stronger than any hatred.'[3] Yet Benjamin's praise here is dialectical, double-edged. It's the master-criminal, after all, who excels at erasing the traces, and this conception of an outlaw aesthetics of modernism coexists alongside an obsession with collecting the traces, the waste-products and detritus, of exactly the oppressive thing-world that 'the new glass-culture' wants to wipe out – in order, as in his excavation of the Paris Arcades, to blow open the historical continuum, to reveal the latent utopia in the covered glass walkways of the recent past. The aim is to wake up out of this dream, with its proliferation of phantasmagorical commodities, into an entirely new world; one shaped by the promises of the dream itself.

There are countless Modernist communiqués and pronouncements that exhibit a sharp distrust of the dreamlike, fantastical city that came about from the hoarding, replication and preservation of the old, something which extends as much to the European streetscape of today as it does to the interiors of the late 19th century. El Lissitzky wrote of

Wyndham Court, Southampton

his Wolkenbügel 'horizontal skyscrapers' that 'the city consists of atrophying old parts and growing, live new ones. We need to deepen this contrast.'[4] This would heighten the contradictions between the new and the old 'atrophied' city, a battle inevitably ending with the death of the latter. Modernism dedicated itself to fighting the old city tooth and nail, as in the famous pronouncement in Marinetti and Sant-Elia's *Manifesto of Futurist Architecture* – 'our houses will last less time than we do, and each generation will have to make its own', a call for 'constant renewal of the architectonic environment'.[5] There's a gulf, certainly, between Benjamin's concern for a revolutionary redemption and the Futurist fetish for inbuilt obsolescence, but both are Modernisms equally hostile to 'heritage'. This is what is meant by erasing the traces – outrunning the old world before it has the chance to catch up with you.

If we want to preserve what remains of Modernism, then we're necessarily conspiring with the very people that have always opposed it: the heritage industries that have so much of Europe in their grip. In the sequence from permanent revolution to preservationism, Modernists have become, according to the late Martin Pawley, 'Quislings'. Pawley wrote in the late 1990s that Modernist Conservation organisations like DOCOMOMO were obliged to 'surrender their modern heritage and agree to its absorption into the art-historical classification system as a style, when it never

5

was. In return they received museum status for many modernist buildings, converting their once-proud revolutionary instruments back into monuments for the delectation of the masses alongside the palaces of the ancien regime...for the promise that part of heritage largesse would in future be spent on the patching up of modernist ruins.'[6] Illustrating Pawley's old believer scorn, DOCOMOMO's chairman Hubert-Jan Henket wrote in their 2000 *Selection from the Registers* that 'Modern buildings belong to the continuity of our civilisation and varied cultures, and must be retained in one form or another for the enjoyment of future generations.'[7] Well, Modernism, in many (if not all) of its manifestations, had no interest in the continuity of our civilisation and the uninterrupted parade of progress. That's why the break in barely ten years between 19th century encrustation and the stark, bare concrete wall was so brutally short and sharp. Not merely 'progress' but an interruption, a rupture, a break with the continuum altogether, regardless of how much it would be slotted back into it later.

Eldorado for the Working Class

> *'What are phenomena rescued from? Not only, and not in the main, from the discredit and neglect into which they have fallen, but from the catastrophe represented very often in a certain strain in their dissemination, their 'enshrinement in the heritage'. – They are saved through the exhibition of the fissure that runs through them. – There is a tradition that is catastrophe.'*
> Walter Benjamin, 'On the Theory of Knowledge, Theory of Progress'[8]

However, Postmodernism's stylistic eclecticism and tendency towards the replica and simulacra complicates memory, to the point where admiring a modernist ruin doesn't just mean filing it away into the historical continuum. I was born in the heavily

Tecton, Bevin Court, London

bombed port of Southampton in the early 1980s, and the city's post-war Modernist buildings would have been finished at least a decade earlier. I can recall looking at its mainly 1960s skyline from the walkway of a bricky pomo Asda, thinking how excitingly modern it all seemed by comparison, a shabby version of the glittering towers of science fiction. Sticking up out of a mass of blandness were extraordinary buildings like Lyons Israel Ellis' Wyndham Court, a council housing block which took the city's contribution to architectural history – the Ocean liner – and Brutalised it into a glorious Concrete Cunard. There were decidedly strange places like Weston Shore, a terminal beach caught between cool 30s pavilions, six monolithic blocks lurking behind scrubland and meadows, all looking out over a gigantic oil refinery. The Weston towers were by the highly prolific city architect, one L. Berger, whose work was singled out for praise in *The Buildings of England* as some of the best post-war building in the country. These varied from the modest and scaled, as in the Northam Estate, to the incongruously enormous Shirley Towers.[9] The mysterious L. Berger also designed the glass and concrete of

7

my secondary school, recently demolished and reconstructed in the PFI style.

It took a while to actually realise the actual age of the city's most recent buildings, as the 1980s were so keen on replicating the 1890s. The environment built before 1979, often being bulldozed and dynamited, seemed so much more futuristic than the houses and interminable shopping malls being built in front of me. Perhaps because of that, concrete walkways and windswept precincts have always seemed to me to have a sharp poignancy. What might be at work here is the common contemporary phenomenon of nostalgia for the future, a longing for the fragments of the half-hearted post-war attempt at building a new society, an attempt that lay in ruins by the time I was born. These remnants of social democracy can, at best, have the effect of critiquing the paucity of ambition and grotesque inequalities of the present.

Caught in the grim paradox of nostalgia for a time yet to come, the utopian imaginary that lies behind any project to remake the world has atrophied. Nevertheless, the word Utopia, after decades of denunciation, has started to re-emerge lately. Not just as a distant, misty-eyed admiration/disdain for the failed ideals of the past, but in the desire to set up perfect, untainted communities of one sort or another. Every gated community dreams of itself as a little island untouched by the hostile, dangerous outside, and the theme park urbanism of Disney towns like Celebration in Florida, abolishing the future in simulation of a fantasy past, aspire to the Ideal.[10] 'The Ideal Home', as the British phrase has it. And appropriately, in London's Docklands, there is now an estate agent called 'UTOPIA'.

The problem, for those who would gladly create a new, if rather less inspiring Modernism on the model of the luxury developments that clog up the banks of the Thames or the Irwell, is that Modernism, in Britain especially, is seen as a remnant of a very different historical conjuncture to that of our own – that embarrassing recent past, the 'interregnum' of Socialism or Social Democracy that we're constantly reminded ended in late-70s chaos. The association was made by many Modernist architects too, although they meant something quite different with it than the much-mytholgised statist dystopia with which it is now eternally linked. In Moscow, there are three council housing blocks which have emblazoned upon them signage which, when read out in full, declares *Glory to the Working Class.*

Ignore for a moment the gauche *Ostalgie* of this, the shabbiness and lies of its political context, and imagine a society where the building of social housing was intended to be exactly that 'glory': an eldorado for the working class, as Berthold Lubetkin once, only half-facetiously put it. The National Housing Service once envisaged by Aneurin Bevan. Then consider the place of council housing in Britain today. As Lynsey Hanley points out in her fine, melancholic history/memoir *Estates*[11], it's now used as shorthand for general lumpenproletarian venality and violence, something for a celebrity to mention when laying out their rags-to-riches credentials. The intriguing thing is that there are two real survivals in present-day Britain of the brief rush of Bevanite Socialism that followed the war: one, the National Health Service, is considered so sacrosanct that even while dismantling it, Tories or New Labour have had to pay it fulsome tributes. The other is the council blocks that still stand all over Britain's cities, monolithically making their point about its essential failure.

Class and politics are inextricably bound up with how a Modernist building is perceived. There is a general conviction that the working class were slotted into a world of concrete walkways and towers when all we ever wanted was the old back-to-backs, with perhaps a little more space, more gardens, maybe without the damp and the dysentery. What can't be imagined is a context in which we might have *welcomed* Modernism, and in fact approached it as part of a specific collective project. The pervasive class hatred only slightly below the surface of British life (what else does the word 'chav' signify?) centres on the feared or ridiculed estate dweller. Yet this decline works both ways. Modernist urban planning could be seen as one of those moments where the workers – the Labour movement – got ideas above its station, the period where , as per Bevan or Lubetkin, nothing was too good for ordinary people.

I lived in a large Estate when growing up, and it was by no means a Modernist one, so the sociologist's links between dehumanised, denatured form and inhuman social effect have always seemed rather too neat, when the same could be produced in a far more traditionalist context. The place in question was a 'cottage estate'; one of those built on the outskirts of cities by councils in the 30s in woolly, vaguely vernacular fashion, with *real homes* featuring *gardens* and *pitched roofs*. Every road was named after a different flower, from carnations to lobelias, in true garden-suburb style. This didn't stop it from being one of the more impoverished, violent and desolate places in Southampton, feared most of all by the students of the nearby University. Proper streets and houses, good old fashioned barbarity – the Flower Estate was much like what is currently being planned for London's Thames Gateway. It couldn't have been further from a Modernist project like Denys Lasdun's Keeling House, laid out as an angular 'cluster block' in order to preserve East End community in the air. Before the block was sold to developers, residents tried to save the building from a demolition threatened by Hackney Council, praising, funnily enough, the 'community' created by the form of the cluster block itself.[12] It's now a *gated* community, a carefully guarded little middle-class utopia.

The absence of events like this from so much Left(ish) urbanism in favour of eulogies to brick is increasingly peculiar, as is the persistence of the belief that because houses were made a certain way in the 19th century, they should continue to be so. Ventures outside of English empiricism just reinforce this, such as in the occasional citing of the Situationists, and specifically their theory of the *dérive*, the 'drift'. A *dérive* was most often in an area that was labyrinthine, inhabited by society's rejected, full of odd corners, frowned upon in Baron Haussman's militaristically planned Paris, a place where you ought to look after yourself: and if there was a certain *nostalgie de la boue* in that, there was also a solidarity with these lost places. If one were to *dérive* anywhere in most British cities, then surely it would be along the concrete walkways of the 60s rather than the gentrified Victoriana?[13] *Estates*, for instance, complains that the complex designs of estates made people get lost, and then that you can't lose yourself in them. 'Too channelled, too labyrinthine to make wandering an enjoyable experience. There's the risk of looking like an intruder, an outsider, or more likely, a wally. You can't be a *flâneur* of the estate, though you are welcome to try'.[14] Ideas above the station again. But from the earliest manifestations of pop culture in the late 40s onwards, working class culture's avant-garde has always been totally, gleefully unafraid of looking like a wally. Ridicule is nothing to be scared of, as Adam Ant so wisely pointed out.

The Tecton group, founded by the Anglo-Soviet architect Berthold Lubetkin, had more organic connection with real rather than imagined working class politics than most, whether working for the miners in Peterlee, with the Labour and Communist councillors of interwar Finsbury, or forming the straightfor- wardly agitational Architects and Technicians Organisation in the '30s as some kind of aesthete-urbanist's wing of the International Brigades. Lubetkin is one of the handful of 'British' Modernists that few have a bad word for, yet his council housing schemes are strangely obscure. These patterned essays in Modernist baroque, such as Spa Green, Bevin Court[15], and Priory Green in Finsbury, Hallfield in Bayswater, or the Cranbrook, Lakeview and Dorset Estates in Bethnal Green: all are as peripheral as their Penguin Pool and Highpoint flats are central to 'classical Modernism'. The Dorset Estate, with its fantastic public areas, such as wild Piranesi staircases, a pod of a library, and a not especially Modernist little

11

boozer, was named after the Tolpuddle Martyrs; among its flats is a block named after the Utopian Socialist Robert Owen. Was this the New Jerusalem for which they had all fought and suffered and died, defeated? Lubetkin claimed, late in life, that 'the philosophical aim and orderly character of these designs are diametrically opposed to the intellectual climate in which we live...my personal interpretation is that these buildings cry out for a world that has never come into being.'[16]

So Modernism is proclaimed, again, to be too good for the worker (or the 'underclass'), and is left for the affluent to play with. Accordingly, in the more prestigious sectors of the neoliberal world, the proclamation of the death of Modernism has proven to be much exaggerated. At least, it has been in architecture, after a 1980s in which everyone from Architectural Association pedagogues to Princes and town planners victoriously put in its place Postmodernism's aesthetic of pastiche, historical reference, cosiness and conservatism. Charles Jencks famously declared Modernism dead on the demolition of Minoru Yamasaki's Pruitt-Igoe housing estate in St Louis, while in Britain it tends to have been dated to the collapse of the shoddy, prole-stacking Ronan Point tower block in East London, in 1972 and 1968 respectively.[17] Regardless: in the first decade of the 21st century, nobody actually designs postmodernist buildings, although they do get built. Urban architecture is dominated by the 'signature' architecture of the Supermodernist star designers, ranging from the Expressionism of Zaha Hadid to the glassy, glossy International Style redux of Norman Foster.[18] However, what most make do with today is building, and in houses, schools and hospitals the choice is between an ultra-timid Ikea Modernism or the semi-Victorian developers' vernacular of Barratt Homes and their ilk. Modernism might have resurged, but in much the same way that a Labour government is no longer a *Labour* government, it isn't quite the same Modernism. This is a Modernism that is based on the distance between itself and the everyday. While the Modern design of the 1920s (in Germany, or the USSR) and the 1960s (in Britain) was immersed in the quotidian, their equivalents today are the designers of corporate skyscrapers, museums and art galleries.

There is another Modernism well worth rescuing from the dustbin of history and the blandishments of heritage. This book is written in the conviction that the Left Modernisms of the 20th century continue to be *useful*: a potential index of ideas, successful or failed, tried, untried or broken on the wheel of the market or the state. Even in their ruinous condition, they can still offer a sense of possibility which decades of being told that 'There is No Alternative' has almost beaten out of us. 'Modernism' here is a rather elastic term, as it always is. It is used here to refer to 20th century arts applied, reproduced and 'fine' (which is why architecture and film, rather than painting and poetry, are central), and an aesthetic deeply immersed in the problems of socialism and psychoanalysis. This isn't to claim that the familiar English Lit 'Right Modernism' is somehow a misnomer, and the two will overlap somewhat in part one's discussion of Wyndham Lewis. The Modernism argued for here is one hostile to the locking of art into the text and the gallery. The distinction this creates between 'high' and 'low' forms is useless for our purposes.

Although much of it will be a study in the aesthetics of architecture and urbanism, the book will digress into film, politics and design, abandoning architecture altogether in the last part. After an opening chapter on the UK, it finds itself in a semi-imaginary Soviet Union, then in Sweden, Yugoslavia, the USA, Germany. The book is divided into four parts, each of which attempts to respond to, attack or play games against a particular critique of Left Modernism. First: *brutality*, via a discussion of the 'brutalist continuum' in Britain. Then onto Modernism's alleged *totalitarian* aspirations, seen through the disparity between the ruined and the futuristic in Soviet Constructivism. The sexlessness that Modernism has so often had apportioned to it is estranged

13

through a reading of the theories and products of *Sexpol*, which, it will be argued, was a key and overlooked element. Finally, the *alienation*, 'detachment' and 'baring of the device' so (over)familiar as a Modernist methodology will be tackled in a piece on Bertolt Brecht's Verfremdungseffekt. The four essays can be read in any order, although the common threads running through should be clear.

The phrase 'erase the Traces' comes from Brecht. Yet in his 'Solidarity Song' he articulated that socialism, though it wants to create a new society, 'lives in traditions', as Leon Trotsky put it. It remembers the defeats, the failed attempts, and with revolution, it enters a world 'already familiar to us, as a tradition and as a vision'[19] Brecht and Eisler's syncopated 'mass song' remembers the pile-up of failures, brutalities and corpses that is politely called history, yet harnesses the memory of those defeats for the purposes of a different world. 'Forwards! Not Forgetting', it implores. This is the outlook that this book tries to maintain.

1: The Brutishness of British Modernism

Aesthetics, modernity and barbarism from Brunel to Bruza

An Englishman's Home is his Fortress

'To be a celebrity you've got to eat the past, nowadays
Who wants to be in a Hovis advert anyway?'
The Fall, 'Just Step S'Ways' (1982)[20]

In 2006, the British chattering classes rediscovered Modernism. Christopher Wilk's V&A exhibition *Modernism – Designing a New World* led, through a survey of interwar Constructivism, Futurism and 'International Style' to a shop selling 'Utopia Soap' and 'Less is More' masking tape. A rash of specials in the 'quality' press, a flurry of publications and TV programmes, made clear that this was an attempt to return to a modernism untainted by its post-war applications in Britain.[21] And indeed, Modernism has not been this accepted in Britain since the 1970s. Yet there is something missing. For instance: Ernő Goldfinger's architecture,

Barratt Homes Modernism at Barrier Point, London

from his Hampstead houses to his Trellick Tower, has never been held in such high esteem. All manner of Notting Hill trustafarians covet a flat in the one-time 'tower of terror', and it's laudable that he was finally proven right about the desirability of high-rise living. Yet the three London buildings of his that were demolished in the 80s and 90s exemplify perfectly what this 'missing' might be. Goldfinger designed a cinema, a Picture Palace, for Oskar Deutsch's pulp modernist Odeon operation, in the Elephant & Castle. He also designed two buildings for the Communist Party of Great Britain, in long since gentrified Clerkenwell and Covent Garden. These absent spaces are exemplars of the two things Ikea Modernism can't abide. First, the crassness and vulgarity of the popular, of mass culture; and second, the unfashionable, uncomfortable class-against-class politics of mass movements.

Perhaps the most irksome of Ikea Modernism's products was Channel 4's *The Perfect Home*, presented by Alain de Botton, promoting his *The Architecture of Happiness*. Perambulating about the place with an expression of casual intellectuality and immense self-satisfaction, he encapsulates all that is malign in British intellectual life. De Botton personifies the faux-naïve stance of the televisual idiot-expert[22], who ventriloquises thinkers from Proust to Boethius to Le Corbusier, emphasising how they can enhance (but certainly never truly change, or question the purpose of) the lives of the administrative classes of terminal capital. In *The Perfect Home* he ponders what architecture *does to our souls* by wafting around the trophy architecture of Berlin's new embassy district, trying to look sardonic in Dubai, and waxing horrified in Thames Gateway Subtopia.

To give him his due, the sections where de Botton talks with a property developer present the face of bovine brit-capital in full force, proudly showcasing their showhome *Heimat*. 'Imagine, going home from work and seeing that, your home, isn't it *lovely*. Nah, if it was built 200 years ago it wouldn't have a built in garage, would it?'[23] A couple in Ipswich are whisked from their tweedy gables to some more modernistically twee housing in the Netherlands, and here the flaw in de Botton's schema is at its most glaring. The choice we are given here is spurious. He exults a vision of sandal-wearing continental modernism, freeze-dried and smug, marked with its timber features and nihilistically blank open plans as Ikea Alvar Aalto, much as the subtopia he rightly mocks is Primark John Nash. It's difficult to miss the hint of condescension beneath the surface here, particularly as he totally sidesteps the question of council housing. Those funny Brits, with their bizarre Mock-Tudor houses! Well, we *had* a Modernism in Britain – not just architectural but musical, artistic, political. It 'failed', but the resentments and conflicts left by that failure are too combustible to be included in de Botton's cosy dichotomy.

The fact unacknowledged, or given one-line dismissals, in the coffee table books and the TV shows is the brief but still very visible dominance Modernism had over British architecture in the 1950s and 60s. The unique (only?) contribution made by Britain to 20th century architecture, as pointed out by Reyner Banham in *The New Brutalism*, was an aesthetic miles from this 'Scandinavian' timidity, and in fact was an earlier response to 'the Swedish retreat from Modern architecture'[24]. On the contrary, it took its lead from the industrial and urban landscapes of the first country in the world to industrialise, fetishising hardness, dynamism, scale and rough edges.[25] As has been pointed out in studies of postwar redevelopment, the city centres of blitzed Britain were given makeovers frequently much more aesthetically extreme than those on the continent – those ferroconcrete fortresses of multi-storey carparks, Arndales and council flats were often the very hardest line Modernism, and were as often the projects of rapacious property developers as those well-meaning old Labour 'paternalists'.[26] They now make up the bulk of programmes like *Demolition*, with their top 10s of concrete carbuncles, a collective groan of 'what were we *thinking*?'

17

Spillers Millennium Mills, London

standing in for thought.

The retreat into let's-pretend newbuild cottages and obsessive makeovers of the old (the grim litany of home improvement programmes, which now make up an entire freeview channel) have to be seen in this context. Accordingly, rather than the jetset smuggery of de Botton, the ideal televisual analogue to the British Modernist aesthetic is probably Fred Dibnah's industrial archae-ology, and his delighted wonder at the future's ruins. Meanwhile, those Brutalist fortresses recall one of the many insufferable clichés about 'Englishness', most likely deriving from an interwar property developer's slogan: that 'an Englishman's Home is his Castle'. Not a cottage, but a *castle*. What is a castle but an unorna-mented, semi-military, functionalist fortress designed to protect its inhabitants? A modern castle would be closer to Alison and Peter Smithson's East End council estate Robin Hood Gardens, setting its face against the thunder of the Blackwall tunnel, sheltering its mainly Bengali tenants from the motorised killing machines and glowering at the shiny corporate shangri-la of

18

Canary Wharf, rather than the Barratt box on the edge of the exurbs.

The Aesthetics of Hell

'(I Recall) Wadsworth taking me in his car on a tour of some of Yorkshire's cities. In due course we arrived on a hill above Halifax. He stopped the car and we gazed down into its industrial labyrinth. I could see he was proud of it. 'It's like Hell, isn't it?' he said enthusiastically.'
Wyndham Lewis, 'Edward Wadsworth'[27]

What we could call the Brutishness of British Art is our subject here. At least as important a component of any 'British' aesthetic as the familiar self-flattery of eccentricity, foppishness or the picturesque is brutality. Roughness, barbarism and a Gradgrindian functionalism have, since the 18th century leap into the unknown, marked much of urban Britain. At a safe temporal distance, the remnants of this might become quaint and lose their power to terrify, but to those who toiled in the Mills that still occasionally survive as prettily alien remnants or loft conversions, they were appalling organisms into whose service they were forced by necessity. The factories and mills of the 19th century took on, after a while, the appearance of temples and palaces, but their true minimalism was always visible at the back, or if in an area sufficiently secluded, on the façade. Nikolaus Pevsner's *Pioneers of Modern Design* features a photograph that proves that Mies van der Rohe's glass grids, that dominate our skylines still, existed in embryo in 1850s Britain in the form of a Sheerness boatstore.[28] And there are reasons other than the hectoring blare of Jeremy Clarkson as to why that poet of iron Isambard Kingdom Brunel was voted second 'greatest Briton' in one of the interminable recent phone plebiscites. Industry and engineering are the things about Britain most likely to survive into the history books 500 years hence – in the event we get that far, given the process of ecological destruction begun by this 'industrial island machine'.

Invention, in the sense of unprecedented products of eccentric geniuses, was not, in fact, the mother of industrial revolution, but rather the brutal application of bastardised technology, creating a bastard people, toiling for anything up to 18 hours and given anatomically improbable tasks. Marx's analysis of the particular effects of this new world upon the workers[29] was modified by Jean-Francois Lyotard a hundred years later into the knowingly extremist claim that this was exactly what they had come to desire, that they relished the violence done to them by the machine. 'In the mines, in the foundries, in the factories, in hell, they enjoyed it, they enjoyed the mad destruction of their organic body which was indeed imposed on them, they enjoyed the decomposition of their peasant identity, the identity that the peasant tradition had constructed for them, enjoyed the disso-lution of their families and villages, and enjoyed the new monstrous *anonymity* of the suburbs and the pubs in the morning and the evening[30]'. The British were the first people to have no contact with the 'soil', were mainly urban by the mid-19th century, and the imaginary return to arcadia can only be understood in this context: as a myth, something longed for because it no longer exists.[31] And although the new world would be dressed up like the mythic Victorian piano legs, that sooner or later its aesthetic qualities would become the object of awed appreciation is unsur-prising. Whether, as per Lyotard, it would be the proletariat itself that would develop these strange new tastes or not, it was certainly they who were the organic matter upon which these experiments were made.[32]

Humphrey Jennings' montage of industrial images *Pandaemonium* places as the very start of the industrial revolution an imagined vision of hell. That is, Milton's description, from *Paradise Lost*, of the building of some sort of hellish factory, 'whose

D Silo, Pontoon Dock, London

griesly top belched fire and rowling smoak'. Importantly, this dates from the defeat of the Republic.[33] Jennings' interpretation of the industrial revolution is that it was what happened instead of the Commonwealth yearned for by the Diggers and the Levellers. For William Blake, proletarian proto-Modernist, in *The Marriage of Heaven and Hell* the inferno was cannier and more emancipatory than the antiseptic heavens, and Milton was 'of the Devil's Party without knowing it'.[34] The Blakean dialectic employed by Jennings enables him to imagine a transfiguration of Hell, and not by sheltering in dreams of heaven. 'Pandaemonium is the palace of all the Devils. Its building began c1660. Its building will never be finished – it has to be transformed into Jerusalem.' Not all of the New Jerusalems that have been proposed have been based on merging heaven and the tilled earth: some have taken the extraordinary forms thrown up in Hell and used them as their starting point.[35]

The modifications made to the working class of the British Isles were also wreaked upon its bourgeoisie, the English

21

Transport Design
CORIN HUGHES-STANTON

Edward Wadsworth, 'Drydocked for Scaling and Painting'

empiricism hardening into Gradgrind's factographic voice, 'inflexible, dry, dictatorial'.[36] An outsider's view can estrange their alleged irregularity, their inability to fit into patterns, hostility to planning, their smug pretensions to non-conformity. Evgeny Zamyatin was a Russian novelist and ex-Bolshevik best known for the 1922 science fiction novel *We*, one of the 20th century's most compelling portrayals of a hell that its inhabitants believe to be heaven. Yet his Taylorist, mathematically organised society is as much an estrangement of England, based on his experience working in Newcastle, as it is of the more obvious totalitarianisms. *The Islanders*, published in 1918, shows the Functionalism of Gradgrind being turned into a vision of all-encompassing scientific management. 'Life', its protagonist claims, 'must become an harmonious machine and with mechanised inevitability lead us to the desired goal'. The 'muddle' that someone like E.M Forster might have seen in Edwardian suburbia is here a mass produced world of interchangeable gents:

> 'The Sunday gentlemen, as is known, were manufactured in one of the Jesmond factories, and on Sunday evenings they appeared on the streets in thousands of copies…all with identical walking sticks and identical top hats, the Sunday gentlemen with false teeth respectably strolled the streets and greeted their doubles.
> Beautiful weather, isn't it?'[37]

'The Great London Vortex': Wyndham Lewis as Chav

*'SOME BLEAK CIRCUS, UNCOVERED, CAREFULLY
CHOSEN, VIVID NIGHT. IT IS PACKED WITH POSTERITY,
SILENT AND UNEXPECTED POSTERITY IS SILENT, LIKE
THE DEAD, AND MORE PATHETIC'*
Wyndham Lewis, *Enemy of the Stars* [38]

In a commonly used art textbook, the entry on Vorticism admonishes that 'brutality is not usually an admirable quality in art, any more than in life'.[39] It is the obvious quality, however, of what was between 1912-20 one of Europe's pioneering abstract art movements (the others being De Stijl and Suprematism). But like the rudeness of *BLAST* and its proto-punk petulance, this aesthetic was too dirty, raw and smoke-blackened for the canons of Modernism that would form in the subsequent decades – the Vorticists had bad manners, yet didn't play the conceptual games that allow people to make careers out of Dada analysis. Like the much-obsessed over contemporary figure of the 'chav', theirs was a style that was, for all its uncouthness and ugliness, essentially rather *neat*. Vorticism, as Wyndham Lewis never tired of explaining, was not a romantic eulogisation of the machine on the Futurist model (which sprang up in then-rural economies like Russia or Italy at the sight of mechanisation for the first time), rather it reflected aesthetic sensibilities that had been warped, 'modified' by the presence of the machine from birth. The process had long been set in motion. The rectilinear atrocities of Vorticism were merely a refusal to (in an inverse of the Futurist gesture) shelter from the industrial surroundings, its harshness unsurprising.[40] Vorticism was a re-imagining of England as the centre of a technological primitivism that would rightfully supersede their Italian Futurist and French Cubist precursors. In Lewis' oft-quoted words to Marinetti: 'you are always on about these driving belts, you are always exploding about internal combustion. We've had machines in England for a donkey's years, they're no novelty to *us*.'[41] This extremely brief movement was dedicated to destroying the fiction that this urban, warlike, ultra-industrialised country was a jolly suburban arcadia.

Vorticism was symptomatic of a supposedly uncharacteristic extremism creeping into English cultural and political life: the Suffragettes' move into direct action, the suppression of revolution in Ireland, and a wave of Trade Union militancy: all of which would find echoes in *BLAST*, the journal of the movement. The 'Blessed' here include the Suffragettes Lillie Lenton and Freda Graham, Ulster Unionist advocate of political violence Edward Carson, and Trade Unionist Robert Applegarth. Note also the blessing of Cromwell, a reminder of how England precedes the continent in its penchant for revolutionary violence. The reproductions in *BLAST* show the style at a peak of metallic propulsion. The Vorticist work of Edward Wadsworth (trained as an engineering draughtsman) is the most intense in its starkness and industrialism, explicitly influenced by the industrial landscape of urban England: the 'industrial island machine' of *BLAST's* manifesto. His 'Newcastle' is pointedly included therein after the blessing of ports. What initially seems like an abstraction entirely without immediate referent often turns out to be a diagram of industrial urbanism: the woodcut 'Mytholmroyd' refers to the Yorkshire village of that name, reducing it to interlocking girders, its unplanned mass a technological landscape of eerily calm beauty, with its central chimney as unifying point.

The 1915 'Abstract Composition' meanwhile veers all the way into Non-Objectivity, its rectilinear contortions and glaring colours suggesting nothing other than the experiments being made by Kasimir Malevich at the same time in Moscow. At this point, the Vorticists and the Suprematists, though it is very unlikely they were aware of each other, had gone furthest into the machine aesthetic that would dominate the avant-garde for the next half century. Put 'Mytholmroyd' alongside much work

Alison and Peter Smithson, Robin Hood Gardens

created 10 years later and it would seem advanced: the early
Wadsworth, and works in *BLAST* 2, such as the propulsive recti-
linear geometry of Jessica Dismoor's 'The Engine', Frederick
Etchells' 'Progression' and Helen Saunders' 'Atlantic City', have
more in common with El Lissitzky's Prouns, the Elementarism of
Theo van Doesburg, the architectural fantasies of Iakov
Chernikhov, than they do with the next 50 years of British art.

This was not necessarily just a formal question either. Vorticist
art excelled at reproduction, at low-cost, low-end, the reduc-
tiveness and grain created by the act of copying: it can be disap-
pointing to see the rather painterly original of one of the xeroxed
ferocities in *BLAST*. Wadsworth's woodcuts like 'Liverpool
Shipping' and 'Drydocked for Scaling and Painting' achieve this
effacing of the original and the organic most impressively, like
episodes from a history of what Lewis Mumford called the
'paleotechnical': the dirty, noisy, lumbering industry of pre-
Fordist, not to mention pre-electronic industrial power. The 1918
'Drydocked' reflects the experience of mechanised war in its
looming, intimidating machinery. Set in an entirely man-made
landscape, the easily penetrated and bruised curves of the human
are entirely absent, reduced to four angular figures applying
'dazzle paint'.[42] The black-lined geometries present an

25

obstructive web. The cheap two-tone starkness, although here once again representational, merely brings into focus the mental images of schematised industry.

This slots in with the Vorticist's eulogising of a kind of technologised primitivism: 'the art instinct is permanently primitive...the artist of the modern movement is a savage (in no sense an 'advanced', perfected, democratic, Futurist individual of Marinetti's limited imagination); this enormous, jangling, fairy desert of modern life serves him as Nature did the more technologically primitive man'.[43] That these woodcuts depicted 'dazzled ships', essentially warships with abstract painting designed to evade the enemy's radar – given a lick of warpaint – is quite apt, and it's telling that this, rather than architecture or industrial design, was where Vorticism merged 'art' and 'life'. Even before the outbreak of war, Vorticism was preoccupied by warfare and the potential for modern man to be reduced to a 'savage' or updated to a robot, and in both cases capable mainly of destruction. Many Vorticist canvases suggest a human body becoming insectoid, eschewing softness for a metallic exoskeleton. Helen Saunders' 1915 'Vorticist Composition (Study for Cannon)' depicts such a figure, adopting the posture of a praying mantis. Atypically, we have here a figure with a recognisable head and limbs, though each is straightened into lines and points. Its 'face' has a single eye, obstructed by stark black. The pink tone of the body suggests flesh in mockery, with the rest of the body attached to a battery of machinery. It resembles Jacob Epstein's contemporaneous 'Rock Drill' or the grand guignol of

Thamesmead

26

Lewis' 'Before Antwerp' (used for the cover of *BLAST* 2) in its proto-Science Fiction qualities of Pulp Modernist machine gothic.

Vorticism shared with Futurism and the avant-gardes that would follow it (Constructivism, De Stijl, Neues Bauen) a desire to change much more than just art practice, to alter the city and everyday life – born of Lewis' permanently conflicting duality of 'art' and 'life', with one or the other becoming supreme at various points – though never quite managing to fuse, unlike his leftist continental successors. These contradictions run through the urbanist treatise *The Caliph's Design*. Here Lewis advocates the effective recon-struction of London along Vorticist principles, recognising that, like Suprematism, Vorticism was essentially an architectonic world. 'We are all perfectly agreed, are we

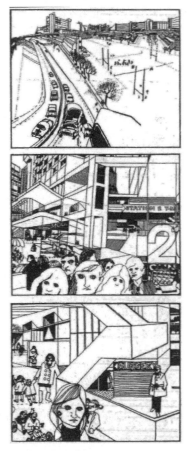

Prospective drawing of Thamesmead

not, that practically any house, railing, monument, wall, structure, thoroughfare, or lamp post in this city should be instantly pulled down..' but for the 'amusement' it provides for the aesthete or the sentimentalist. Although the rhetoric at times seems Constructivist, it always stops short of their collectivism, although the haughtiness is tempered rather by the stated preference for George Formby over Soutine. 'Architecture is the weakest of the arts, in so far as it is the most dependent on the collective sensibility of the period…if the world would only build

27

temples to machinery in the abstract then everything would be perfect.' The end result is much the same, however – a use of the machine not as subject, but as vocabulary, 'a new resource, as if it were a new material or oil'.[44]

To see what happened instead of the Vorticist reconstruction of London, or the urbanist projects that Lewis' former comrades in abstraction created in Holland or the USSR, go to Aldwych and Kingsway, much of which was built in neoclassical style in the 1920s. Turning from the tube station into High Holborn, you will find a (now rather unremarkable) office block. Designed by Frederick Etchells, a signatory of the Vorticist manifesto, this was the first rigorously Modernist (as opposed to art deco) building in London, as late as 1930. Etchells was the translator of Le Corbusier's *Vers une Architecture*, and it's notable how, for the next decade, the avant-garde would be an importation with the wave of émigrés post-1933. The British adaptation of it into something as distinctive as its forbears was already forgotten. At 1920's 'Group X', the last Vorticist exhibition, Wadsworth exhibited a speculative sculpture, a plan for a Vorticist building. It was an almost formless but austere concrete fist, with a wrought, tactile surface, impenetrable and alien. It might not have been built in the 20s and 30s, but structures much like it would turn up in English cities not long after. Vorticism, as Lewis stated when surveying the tentative Modernism of 30s Britain, 'was aimed essentially at an *architectural* reform...(Vorticist pictures) were often rather exercises in architectural theory – rather pictorial *spells*, as it were, cast by us, designed to attract the architectural shell that was wanting – than anything else.' For the Vorticist the clean, antiseptic Modernism resulting from the early adaptations of Corbusier *et al* was also wanting. 'You should not be afraid of *desecrating* these spotless and puritanic planes and prudish cubes.' But the shell would arrive soon enough.[45]

The Greater London Council Vortex: A Bit of the Old Ultraviolence

'Where I lived was with my dadda and mum in the flats of municipal flatblock 18A, between Kingsley Avenue and Wilsonway. I got to the big main door with no trouble, though I did pass one young malchick sprawling and creeching and moaning in the gutter, all cut about lovely, and saw in the lamplight also streaks of blood here and there like signatures, my brothers, of the night's fillying.'
Anthony Burgess, *A Clockwork Orange*[46]

There was soon enough a movement that would desecrate the puritanic plane. We could call it, with a nod to their precursors, 'the LCC (or from the '60s on, GLC) Vortex': the aesthetic of London's metropolitan government before its 1980s abolition. The product of a Social Democratic institution rather than Vorticism's marginalised Bohemians. This aesthetic was one of two architectural responses to the aftermath of the Second World War, and the attendant determination to break with the shabbiness of aesthetic and political laissez-faire.[47] There was the Aalto-influenced Scandinavian softening of Modernism exemplified by the new towns and the Festival of Britain; and another, more controversial movement: what was christened in the early 1950s as 'the New Brutalism'. The phrase comes from a variety of possible sources, whether the jibes of 'Swedish', 'empiricist' architects, Peter Smithson's nickname, and perhaps most importantly, *béton brut*: raw, reinforced concrete, without render, without façade, not smoothly filed down but allowed to stay rough, or textured by shutters and bush-hammers. A material both futuristic and primal. This is something worth remembering, seeing as it became by the 70s a general synonym for all that was inhuman and obnoxious in urbanism. Béton Brut may have been a French invention, pioneered for Le Corbusier's micro-phalanstery, the

The Barbican

Unité d'Habitation, but as a material it found its greatest expression in Britain, where the climate was all too ready to provide the staining and weathering. The two factions even designed competing ends of the London County Council's *Ville Radieuse* at Roehampton, the Alton Estate.

The New Brutalists, as Banham defined them in 1955, were an architectural analogue to the 'angry young men', known also to be of 'redbrick extraction' and a product of the new class mobility: only with their abstraction cancelling out the blokeish peevery of their literary contemporaries. Brutalism thrived on a dialectic of the purist and the fragmented, montage and the memorable single image. If their opponents were Stalinist, Brutalism was Trotskyist: while opposing the practice of the 'masters' of 'classical' modernism, it supported the original theory in toto and regarded itself as the fulfilment rather than the abolition. Alison and Peter Smithson were only the most famous of the 'angry young London

30

architects', with their affection for warren-like slum streets, science fiction and 'bloody-minded' form[48]: the LCC architects of Alton West, the designers of Lambeth tower blocks, the Sheffield City Council planners of Park Hill, faceless firms like Lyons Israel Ellis and Owen Luder Partnership...The paradox of Brutalism was its intent to at once produce an earthy, everyday style for the use of the proletariat (one where they wouldn't have to mind their manners inside) and at the same time create avant-garde, shocking images, to be 'a brick-bat flung in the public's face'.[49] Yet the Smithsons themselves were Pop Artists, of a sort: members of the Independent Group and inveterate collectors and connoisseurs of consumerist detritus. Alison Smithson wrote of their 'House of the Future', an all-plastic experiment of 1956, that 'the overall impression given to the public should be one of glamour'.[50]

In the early 1950s the Smithsons produced a housing project for a bombsite in the City of London. Rather than illustrating their project with isometric drawings, they produced a photomontage – a design of their new building with its internal streets and angular, austere forms – and imposed on them discrete cut-out figures. Some seem to be having gun-fights, others are running, all seem possessed by a distinct energy, far from the calm Platonism of the international style. Among the montaged figures are those of mid 20th century hyper-celebrity. In the foreground Marilyn Monroe and Joe DiMaggio are ducking, huddled as if running from paparazzi. The Golden Lane project, polemically debated at the Congres International d'Architecture Moderne in 1956[51], can be seen as both a highpoint and repudiation of British Modernism. While it innovates furiously, and participates in debates started by Le Corbusier's streets in the Unité d'Habitation, it is fundamentally an attack on the purism and anti-urbanism of their predecessors. They would centre on the street, rather than spaced, radiant blocks in repetitive rows, or for that matter the picturesqueness of the garden cities, which were Britain's last contribution to a new urbanism. Their development would be dense, it would be urban, and while it would unashamedly house the poor, be part of the new Welfare State, it would be *glamorous*.

In short, it would be Pop. An architectural equivalent to their colleague in the Independent Group Richard Hamilton's montage *What is it that makes today's homes so different, so appealing?* with its images of consumer technology, Americanism and easy-access eroticism. An architecture both of austerity *and* abundance, in line

Eros House, Catford

with the contradictions of the post-1945 melange of Socialism and Capitalism that created the post-war boom. Accentuating the most fertile features of both. At the same time it furnished the form of one of the most radical critiques of the post-war settlement, as the streets in the sky were borrowed by the Situationists' New Babylon project, a city to be built on the ruins of social democracy's fudges and compromises.[52] It's a perfect example of Brutalism's preference for the 'as found'. It merely takes the gallery-access system of walk-up LCC flats of the 20s/30s, such as Edwin Lutyens' extraordinary checkerboard Grosvenor Estate, and re-imagines it as a site of Pop Utopia.

The Smithsons' 'Criteria for Mass Housing' was a ruthless critique of 'classical' Modernism, in a series of pointed, cruel questions: from 'can the individual add 'identity' to the house, or is the architecture packaging him?' to 'is the development isolated – would it look like a camp?'[53] By implication, the orthodoxies of the international style failed this criteria, but theirs, presumably, would not. Other than Park Hill, Sheffield, the built version of this is at Robin Hood Gardens, the late 1960s development where the Smithsons finally had free rein to build their streets in the sky, the name suggesting an actual and conceptual robbing from the rich for the benefit of the poor. It's undeniably impressive. Fortress-like, daringly sculptural, with its gradated concrete gleaming golden in the sun – a building that might have evoked glamour if the setting were not so dispiriting, next to the thunderous Blackwall tunnel, the grim reality of fifties Autopia. Two networks of internal streets and flats, this was what they called 'building for the socialist dream, which is something different from simply complying with a programme written by the socialist state', a structure as 'dramatic and obvious as an aqueduct', the 'theme' of which was 'protection'.[54] Robin Hood Gardens *looks* like a stronghold, but one can't imagine anyone defending it right now. Around six miles west is the Smithsons' famous ensemble of buildings for *The Economist*: building for the capitalist reality, elegant and impeccably up-kept, a quiet enclave rather than an embattled encampment. Robin Hood Gardens is the sort of social housing that *The Economist* would abhor, a stain on the architects' reputation. A 'sink estate', passed over with unseemly haste in the many academic discussions of the Smithsons' work. It won't stay obscure for long, though, seeing as it borders the huge new town for finance capital at Canary Wharf. Demolition has just been proposed at the time of writing.[55]

Brutalism is not the same thing at the centre as it is at the periphery. There's a huge, windswept distance between the Barbican, on the edge of the Medieval walled city, by the old Cripplegate, and Thamesmead, on the edge of the 19th century metropolis, a two-hour bus ride from its heart. Here we have two absurdly similar projects. Built in the 60s and 70s, both ran way over budget, both employed a counterpoint between reinforced concrete and placid artificial lakes, and both are strangely quiet, the tall buildings isolating them from traffic noise. Yet they couldn't be more different. The fierce beauty of one is still used for video shoots to represent urban anomie. The facilities promised in the original plan – what the planners called, pointing to the mundane-utopian tension, 'the visionary basic approach'[56]: cinemas, repertory theatre and ice rink, not to mention the tube station – never arrived, and before being sold off the plans were scrapped and replaced with 'neo-vernacular' cottages. The Barbican had all its facilities completed, eventually, and now houses stockbrokers and intellectuals (though was once home to Arthur Scargill and an exiled Benazir Bhutto), a chattering class arts centre, and an atmosphere of ease and comfort.

Round the corner from Golden Lane, where a more sober project that beat the Smithsons' still stands, the Barbican is one of the most obvious vindications of their theories. A recent tourist guide describes this complex, designed by Chamberlin, Powell and Bon over a nearly 20 year period, as a 'monumental concrete ghetto'. And, if one tries to ignore the wealth of the inhabitants, this is what we have here. Three utterly enormous towers, the largest residential buildings in Europe at the time: curves and spikes, carrying excitement and a hint of fear – and lower but no less fierce blocks curving round some showpiece lakes, linked by a series of seemingly endless walkways, under and overpasses and Smithsonian streets in the sky. Rather than intimidating and bleak, the Barbican is as attractive and mysterious as a J.G Ballard heroine. This isn't entirely an accident. The Barbican was not built as social housing, and its inhabitants are comfortable enough to be able to handle the old ultraviolence.

More important, in terms of actually vindicating Modernism as creator of socialist spaces, is the relative failure of Thamesmead, a failure that seems somehow more noble than the Barbican's success. The bus to get there drops you off somewhere in-between two monuments to Blairism – the barbaric Belmarsh Prison (brick, of course) and further to the East, the Bluewater shopping centre. Then you arrive somewhere which, even nominally, is a memorial to post-war Social Democracy: one enclave has roads called Attlee,

Keynes, Applegarth, and as if to confirm Burgess' fears, a Harold Wilson House. Of course, this vast estate is most famous as one of Kubrick's locations in the 1972 film of *A Clockwork Orange*.[57] A signifier of Modernism become perverse and violent, brutalism in the material sense transliterated into physical brutality. The buildings – white-grey concrete point blocks linked by walkways to lakes and futuristic low-rise maisonettes – seem as cold, stylish and psychotic as Alex and his droogs. But over thirty years later, Thamesmead doesn't look violent, so much as melancholy. A 2005 project on Thamesmead by Susanna Round and Rachel Barbaresi[58] shows it becoming successful in the sense that it has inspired a sense of the territorial: the planners' logo is used as graffiti all over the area, while the inhabitants have painted mock-Tudor panels onto the reinforced concrete, the 'sense of identification' spoken of in the original project brief.

The lakes and canals, which the brief suggested could mean 'one of the pleasures in store for future residents may be Saturday shopping by boat' are full of rare birds, patiently waiting for their eventual reclamation of the site. Thamesmead is ringed by private developments, built in the historical pick & mix of the Thatcherite/Blairite era, which try and abolish history in their determined traditionalism. When one of the central areas was demolished in 2006 a local press headline declared 'NO MORE CLOCKWORK ORANGE', reminding that the place is still defined by its fictionalisation. Imagine the same happening to Clough Williams-Ellis' Portmeirion, chosen by Patrick McGoohan as set for *The Prisoner*, a nightmarish vision of middle class English politesse and tweeness running a surveilled mini-state. This collage of Lewis Carroll Italianate structures is the setting for something every bit as terrifying as Kubrick's dystopia, yet for North Wales' press to cry 'NO MORE PRISONER' upon its mutilation would be inconceivable. This isn't just because the inhabitants of one live there out of choice and those of the other out of necessity. Portmeirion, rather than Thamesmead, accords with how the British like to see themselves: eccentric, individualist, nostalgic. *The Prisoner* prefigured postmodern urbanism, in that its pretty cottages mask an ultra-modern interior of advanced information technologies, while its cul-de-sacs are littered with surveillance cameras. Portmeirion is a tourist destination, while Thamesmead is a notorious estate. Yet both settlements are equally weird, obsessive and beautiful.

Everyone on Park Hill came in unison at 4.13 AM

'There is something aphrodisiacal about the smell of wet concrete.'
Denys Lasdun[59]

England loves the 1960s: its indie rock obsesses over a retread of a retread of the last time it seemed internationally significant, its populace yearn for the 1966 of *Revolver* and being good at football, the haircuts and the Bond films become perennial. The exception to this is in architecture, which is interesting, seeing as it was at the time considered so much a part of this brief moment of Modernist, technocratic optimism. Architecture, unlike the other arts, can't be ignored, can't be passively consumed, not if you have to *live* in it. A close equivalent to Brutalism's avant-garde quotidian is in the work of the BBC Radiophonic Workshop. Banham makes a more than punning connection between the techniques of concrete brutalism and those of *musique concrete*, in that both are based on the use of manipulated found objects, both have a disdain for harmony but not for structure[60]. The Workshop applied *musique concrete* to TV jingles, soundtracks, mundane everyday sound. What made both so valuable is that they were so totally immersed in everyday life. Switch on the radio or walk out of the door to find yourself in a new world.

Yet Brutalism was still in some definable relation to pop and the sexual revolution, or the 'permissive society' as it was more coyly described. One of the most admired early brutalist

Ferrier Estate, Kidbrooke

buildings was the Owen Luder Partnership's Eros House, a mixed-use concrete and glass arrangement of geometric conflicts, its name a reminder of the strangely lubricious tone that occasionally creeps into this aesthetic. The most remarkable testament to the sexuality of the Streets in the Sky is on Pulp's 1993 singles collection *Intro*. Therein is a 10 minute fantasia called 'Sheffield: Sex City', in which every contour and line of the industrial city is filled with eroticism. It begins with a deadpan Yorkshire voice (keyboardist Candida Doyle), reading out a Nancy Friday tale about an adolescent girl living in a block of flats, who would 'lie there mesmerised' as the entire tower seemed to come on heat. Then, to a metronomic disco pulse, Jarvis Cocker recites a list of Sheffield suburbs with luridly sensual relish, then finds himself searching the city for his lover, driven to 'making love to every crack in the pavement'. The whole ludicrous, astonishing construction eventually comes to a climax of utopian urbanist carnality, as 'everyone on Park Hill came in unison at 4.13am, and the whole block fell down'.[61]

Park Hill, with its endless walkways and Constructivist/

Brutalist intersections and permutations, exemplifies the truly visionary potentialities of the post-war moment perhaps better than any other structure, its vaulting over-ambitiousness almost ensuring that the inhabitants never had to touch the ground. To eroticise such a structure isn't much of a rhetorical leap – think of the geometries of Ballard's architecturally-obsessed *Atrocity Exhibition*, in which the intersection of two walls is as erotic as that of two legs, and where the abstraction of Brutalism is transliterated into mental and sexual landscapes. This is amply symbolised in Jack and Chamian Seward's 1974 propaganda film for the Greater London Council, *Living at Thamesmead*.[62] The innocence and hope of this utopia of the slum overspill is personified in the pubescent protagonists, bathed in the sunlight that reflects off the concrete surfaces. Opening with scenes of the communal lakes turned, seemingly, into Butlins, filled with frolicking children, we move onto a walk through the gigantic estate, soundtracked by a bucolic electro-acoustic ditty that demands reissue on Trunk Records. The couple can't keep their hands off each other: at one point they lie in an embrace on the playing fields. The camera closes in on the girl's red, parting lips, then dissolves. Their traversal of the concrete walkways is at every level sexualised, their fictionalised kitchen-sink romance made symbolic of the appeal of the sparkling, *ex nihilo* city. Inevitably, the film ends with the couple deciding to move there to raise a family...

What's funny, and sad, is that even in this film, made purely to convince people to move to the estate, the tenants' complaints (justified, no doubt) are so central, and so familiar. There's not enough facilities. The rent is too high. It's too isolated. The public transport isn't good enough. What isn't mentioned, except by allusion, is the architecture, and the sheer confidence and total sweep of its Modernism (the directors not chastened by *A Clockwork Orange* two years before). At one point the boy looks over to the school and exclaims 'it looks like a factory!' and the girl replies 'better than my old one. *Old* was the word for it!' The very things that are now considered so inhuman, so criminal about Thamesmead and its lesser versions – the walkways, the towers, the concrete, the lack of any ornament or historicist 'context' (context with what? The poisoned wasteland that was there before?) – are not considered worthy of comment by the people in the film, both those fictional and real. The camera, meanwhile, adores the architecture, and the directors have the characters acknowledge it, silently: as at one moment across the walkways, where our couple turn back to see the geometries line up starkly behind them, a row of gradated towers stepping back, one after the other. A glance that would now have to be one of fear is of wonder.

Mark Owens has written of a 'delayed reaction'[63] causing the aesthetic effects of the New Brutalism on many of its inhabitants to have only really become apparent in the Pop of the late 1970s, where after a time they were able to produce something as strange, inhuman and futuristic as the architecture. The bastard technologies and deadpan dystopianism of Cabaret Voltaire and the early Human League (declaring 'high rise living's not so bad' in 1979, the year that the Tories declared an intention to 'tear down the tower blocks'[64]) are New Brutalism in Pop, much as the latter was Pop in architecture: the rough synth textures, the bastardised technologies and outlook caught between techno-logical optimism and urban paranoia. Japan, straight out of Catford, sang of the romance of 'concrete squares' and 'east Berlin', John Foxx's Ultravox declared that 'my sex is invested in suburban photographs/skyscraper shadows on a car crash overpass...my sex is an image lost in faded films/a neon outline on a car crash overspill'.[65] For many post-punk currents, Brutalist imagery was not so much source for socialist realist critique as a spur to new conceptions of surface and space.

Since then, the only serious signs of Britain's continued cultural life have been clearly brutalist-indebted: that is, what

Simon Reynolds has called the 'Hardcore Continuum'[66], the bastardisations and misappropriations of Black American form that have emerged from multiracial estates. The original Hardcore, the chaotic, cheap mutation of techno that was prominent in the early 90s, was treated by purists in much the same fashion as Vorticism was regarded by Cubist and Futurist scholars – illegitimate, and as vulgar and pugnacious as a brutalist block. The mutations of this, transmitted over the airwaves from the tops of tower blocks, have themselves created further new forms: jungle, 2-step, grime, bassline house. Watch the 'urban' music station Channel U to see how the British are still the Brutish. After a series of seamless, smooth American videos you might be confronted with the deadpan humour, aggression and love of cheap technology that characterise what, tweaking Reynolds, we could call The Brutalist Continuum. What still marks out British Art[67] is essentially a certain *crapness*, a refusal of ease and slickness in favour of angularity and harshness, and subtlety always repudiated in favour of the instant, Pavlovian response, the organic with the artificial. 'Brutal and British', as the grime MC Bruza declares himself in his stentorian bellow.

Future Ruins

'There are deep-seated instincts which will beat functionalism in the end'.
Sir Reginald Blomfield, *Modernismus* (1934)[68]

The 1950s-70s' 'cities in the sky' are (as mentioned earlier) in the first decade of the 21st century, along with the NHS, the most persistent remnant of British Socialism. A constant danger is that the aesthetic argument can be used as a smokescreen for the political. Park Hill, once regarded as one of the few examples of hardline municipal socialist modernism to have 'worked', has recently been subject to a regeneration programme. As so often

Ferrier Estate, Kidbrooke

with such schemes, the beautification of an inner-city working class area is achieved by removing its inhabitants. The privatisation of one of the century's greatest public projects is covered by a fevered argument – is an eyesore? Is it a masterpiece? The question so seldom asked is what the residents think. Regardless of their aesthetic opinions, tenants frequently want to stay in their council flats, and this is precisely the option that isn't on the table. A similar process is enacted all over Britain: the selling-off and demolition of public housing is presented as a philanthropic gesture. A typical report, Greenwich Council's plan for the Ferrier Estate in Kidbrooke, South London, advocates demolishing the 'discredited' brutalist towers, walkways and streets in the sky. The density will then be more than doubled, the land sold off, most of the remaining inhabitants chucked out, and the affluent shipped in. The plan accompanying the 'consultation', states with inadvertent poignancy that 'there was no sense of ownership in the communal areas'.[69] Meanwhile, those tenants who have refused to take the council's (meagre) financial incentives to leave now reside in an enormous, derelict *Ville Radieuse* turned wasteland, resembling the Soviet towns left rotting after Chernobyl.

Council tenants have shown a tendency to vote down the incessant ballots imploring them to sell up. Far be it for us to suggest that this might be because they actually like the views and the open space.[70] Curiously enough, for an aesthetic so often blamed for demolishing the warren-like streets and rookeries, the remnants of brutalism are in the popular imagination precisely what the old slums always were – places of crime and intrigue, places where you could easily get lost, where strange people do strange things, and from whence revolt and resistance might just emerge. Perhaps this merely proves their failure. Yet as the Disneyfication of Britain continues apace, the walkways, towers, and concrete surfaces are all we have left, the only thing standing in the way of gentrification's purge of undesirables from urban space. Brutalism, with its rough-hewn rawness, always was a vision of future ruins. This shouldn't console those who always hated it, however. The ruined is dead, safe, and can be regarded with relieved disdain. Brutalism is not so much ruined as dormant, derelict – still functioning even in a drastically badly treated fashion, and as such ready to be recharged and reactivated. This rough beast might still slouch towards a concrete New Jerusalem.

2: A Hole into the Future

Space Exploration and Excavation in Soviet Modernism

Red Planet Mars

"This is a hole. It always has been and still is. But now it is a hole into the future. We're going to dump so much through this lousy hole into your world that everything will change in it. Life will be different. It'll be fair. Everyone will have everything he needs. Some hole, huh? Knowledge comes through this hole. And when we have the knowledge, we'll make everyone rich, and we'll fly to the stars, and go anywhere we want. That's the kind of hole we have here."

Arkady & Boris Strugatsky, *Roadside Picnic*[71]

There is a Cold War B-Movie of the 1950s which depicts the nearest, 'red' planet of the Solar System as a hive of filthy Commies.[72] Aficionados of such things will know this isn't as silly as it sounds. The history of Martian Marxism begins in 1908 with a novel by Bolshevik theorist, scientific-artistic tinkerer and future leader of the Proletcult ('proletarian culture') movement, Alexander Bogdanov. In *Red Star* a young socialist is transported to an achieved Socialism on Mars, inadvertently predicting the notoriously bizarre 'Posadist' Trotskyists.[73] Yet H.G Wells' original Martians are, it should be remembered, a fantasy of anti-imperialist revenge. Wells was outraged by the British Empire's extermination of the aboriginal population of Tasmania, and his alien invasion is a way of inflicting the very same treatment – obliteration by a more technologically advanced society – upon the West. In this sense, it's not quite so surprising that one of the war cries of the Russian Futurists was *War of the Worlds'* Martian roar 'ULL-AA', which would in 1919 provide the title for one of

Viktor Shklovsky's manifestos for the alienation effect, 'Ullya, Ullya, Martians'. In order to truly *estrange*, to provide the distance from everyday life's stock responses and learned indifference that, for Shklovsky, is the key element in great literature, art, or the circus, the alienation effect is taken literally to mean the visitation by the alien nation. Shklovsky writes of an avant-garde work being 'worthy of my brothers, the Martians'[74]. This is how much of the Russian Avant-Garde saw themselves – like Tatlin's Third International Tower, whose iron legs and perpetual motion are

akin to the Martians' walking tripods, this was something as fearsome, uncanny and technologically terrifying as the alien invasion, and intended to be every bit as threatening to existing society.

A history of the Soviet avant-garde could be written through its aspirations to the interstellar.[75] It would run through, after Shklovsky or Velimir Khlebnikov's 'Trumpet of the Martians', to Iakov Protazanov's 1924 film *Aelita, Queen of Mars.* This was one of the first Constructivist built environments, housing a Martian despotism that the earthlings bring to revolution. The set by Isaac Rabinovich is made up of sharp glass polygons, with Alexandra Exter's costumes adding an inorganic sexuality to the proceedings. In fact, the schlock aesthetics of robots and martians as depicted in *Aelita* proves that both the B-Movie and cyberpunk have roots in Constructivism. We could go from there to Georgy Kriutikov's Flying City, a comprehensive plan for an architecture capable of travelling through the air; or Kasimir Malevich's Planity, an abstract interstellar architectonics made up of his exploded Suprematist squares and rectangles.

Still from Aelita, directed by Yakov Protazanov

Even the Soviet space programme, long after the vanquishing of the avant-garde, fulfils many of these utopian promises. [76]

In that case, one could look at the remnants of the avant-garde project that litter the former USSR as the detritus left by the Martians. The incomprehensible, incommensurable ruins of a strictly temporary visitation by creatures not like ourselves. The Strugatsky Brothers' tremendous 1972 novel *Roadside Picnic* depicts the aftermath of such an event. A city that has been 'visited' is left with the Zone in the area where the visitation took

Mission to Mars, poster by Nikolai Prusakov & G.I Borisov

place: a fenced-off, contaminated and ruined area, marked by scatterings of the bizarre and technologically fantastic objects left by the alien visitors. The Zone is a dangerous, melancholy place, an industrial district where the chimneys no longer give off smoke, visited by strange climactic phenomena, with a stretched sense of time. Within it, however, is quite literally the answer to all human wishes, something which in the last instance holds the promise of eternal happiness for all humanity.

Filmed by Andrei Tarkovsky in 1979 as *Stalker*, the Zone is visualised as a Chernobyl-like scarred, postindustrial landscape of ruins, waste, rubbish, of the remnants of industrial civilisation corroded, dilapidated and rapidly being reclaimed by nature. Tarkovsky's version of the Zone has gradually, over the last thirty years, become the foundation of an entire aesthetic. If Modernity, or Modernism, is our Antiquity, then its ruins have become every bit as fascinating, poignant and morbid as those of the Greeks or Romans were to the 18th century. Tarkovsky's Zone is in some ways specific to the former USSR and in particular a few locations in Estonia, yet practically every industrial, or once industrial country, has something resembling the Zone within it. Such an area would be, for instance, the remnants of industrial districts of East London. Beckton, Woolwich, Stratford, places marked by the cyclopean remains of silos, gasometers, factories, and scatterings of overambitious social housing, with their crumbling towers and walkways. These are remnants of something as alien and incomprehensible to the seamless mallscape of 21st century Capital, or the heritage Disneyland of European Urbanism, as Shklovsky's Futurist Martians were to their contemporaries: only here without any of the insurrectionary promise of a new world, merely the ruins of an old one.

Theories of Ruin Value

'Half ruined buildings once again take on
The look of buildings waiting to be finished
Generously planned: their fine proportions
Can already be guessed at: but they still
Need our understanding. At the same time
They have already served, indeed have already been overcome. All this
Delights me.'
Bertolt Brecht, 'Of All the Works of Man'[77]

So we have here, via these two models of alien visitations in the imagination of Russian Modernists, whether of the 20s or the 70s, two competing models of Modernity. On the one hand, the advancing, gleaming, ruthless aesthetics of Futurism, particularly, for our purposes here its mutation into the more humanist, politicised Constructivism. On the other, an aesthetic of disintegration, of the aforementioned Futurist world's gradual descent into an overgrown, poisoned wasteland. Both are, of course, spaces that can be found easily enough in any 'developed' country, and both represent an aesthetic with both revolutionary and reactionary elements.

Richard Pare, Baku Palace of the Press

This divide is presented most poignantly in the architectural photographer Richard Pare's magnificent project *The Lost Vanguard*. Selected out of an archive of 10,000 photographs, this is a documentation of Modernist architecture in the USSR from 1922 to 1932. Pare approaches the subject matter like the Strugatsky brothers' Stalkers, making journeys into the dilapidated working class quarters of the former Soviet Republics, bargaining for passes into military-industrial sites, and returning with depictions of exquisite objects that have, quite clearly, seen better days. The book is the final meeting point of the two poles of the Soviet Modernist aesthetic – the gleaming, seamless surfaces, revolutionary optimism and technocratic zeal having long since been overtaken by weathering, their concrete cracked, their artificial, glaring paintwork faded and crumbling and the technical rhetoric shown to conceal medieval construction techniques. Yet the archaeological scale of Pare's project is equally remarkable: an

47

entire illustrated history of a country's Modernist architecture, which easily rivalled in its formal brilliance and the totality of its scope the 'classical Modernist' (and very well maintained) German and Dutch work of the 1920s and 30s.

At the start of T.J Clark's *Farewell to an Idea*, the author imagines a series of Modernist relics being chanced upon by an archaeologist: a Picasso, Adolphe Menzel's sketch 'Moltke's binoculars', and most interestingly for us, a photomontage by John Heartfield for the *Arbeiter Illustrierte Zeitung*, a German language Communist Party glossy. This, 'New Man, Master of a New World', was in celebration of 17 years of the USSR. A huge, weathered face, with tears in its eyes, is centre of a photomontaged landscape of industry, mass mobilisation and Modernist architecture – some collective housing blocks, and the newly built 'Palace of the Press' in Baku. This near-incomprehensible montage would nonetheless speak of Modernism's poignancy, its political commitment, and its harnessing itself to a highly ambiguous industrial modernity. 'No doubt, the Baku Palace of the Press, if it survives, is as overgrown and labyrinthine as Shelley's dream of Rome.' [78]

Well, Pare has been to the Baku Palace of the Press, designed by Semen Pen in 1932 and now in Azerbaijan, and several pages of *The Lost Vanguard* are devoted to it. [79] In fact, it's one of the better preserved of the buildings: its render might be chipping off, and the interiors are stained and filled with seemingly random piles of burnt-out rubbish, but unusually it's still a working plant, and the building's silhouette with its dynamic, curved balconies and roof garden looks as impressive in Pare's photographs as in Heartfield's montage. Elsewhere though, this is a tale of utter devastation. A few pages later, again in Baku, is the Shaumian Settlement, a workers' housing project: described by Pare as 'relatively well preserved'. [80] A more astonishing Modernist wasteland would be difficult to find: huge swathes of the blocks stained and rotting, with a blasted hole at the centre, yet the ambitiousness of the settlement is still visible: jutting, curved loggias, a bright, imaginative colour scheme, a clear-eyed promise of *ex nihilo* Socialist Modernism. Or a couple of pages after that, there's two Workers' Clubs by Leonid Vesnin in the same city: stark, sheer faces of blank render broken up by tiny windows and curved stair towers. Abandoned, both of them look entirely alien: Modernist and almost medieval in their simplicity, seemingly without architectural precedent, and left to the mercies of the elements. As in the Zone, time goes haywire: they could have been there forever as much as they appear to have been designed last week.

In contemplating these images however, one is reminded of the interesting element to Albert Speer's otherwise utterly banal 'Theory of Ruin Value'. Not the bluster over the impressiveness of ancient ruins, and the need to leave similarly imposing remains. Rather, the psychotic, suicidal notion of building with the ruins already in mind: a death-drive architecture, where posterity's opinion is internalised to such a ludicrous degree that, in a sense, the corpse has been designed before the living body. Pare's introduction makes a point which touches on this Speerian madness when he describes chancing upon the carcass of a Factory Kitchen in St Petersburg, designed by architects from the avant-garde group ASNOVA. Every single part of it that can be has been taken for scrap, from windows to steel reinforcement: in an especially *Stalker*-esque moment, the photographer disturbs a group of people sat around a fire made up of the building's remains. The gutted carcass, he points out, finally resembles the architects' original concept. Bereft of the adverts, additions and disfigurements imposed on many other structures, this is the Platonic form of the building, as much as it would have been in the original drawings, the purity of the death mask's lines more clear than those of the living building would be. This, the implication might be, was its inevitable final form. Alas, such a notion is entirely false: Constructivist architecture made a fetish of the extraneous, and adverts, banners or radio masts can be found as features of

Richard Pare, Shaumian Workers Club

most of the original plans.[81] In fact, the chaotic advertising that blocks out the lines of the original buildings is closer to the original impulse than is the urge to preserve.

Nonetheless, there's another archaeological element here which points to this book's huge importance for the history of what, with appropriately Homeric epithets, is generally known today as 'heroic' or 'classical' Modernism. This is the most comprehensive documentation of the legacy of Constructivist architecture ever published in the English language, and has a good claim to be the most complete produced anywhere else. Yet, Jean-Louis Cohen's historiography of the period makes clear that at the time they were built, these were objects of proud, and successful, propaganda. Leading western Modernists were subscribers and sometimes contributors to Soviet architectural publications like *ASNOVA News* or *SA* (Contemporary Architecture). Soviet developments were at the heart of the early

50

Congres International d'Architecture Moderne, and the Soviet Union was generally seen as the only serious rival to Weimar Germany in the intensity of its experimentation. Books such as Bruno Taut's *Modern Architecture*, Adolf Behne's *Der Moderne Zweckbau*, Karel Teige's *The Minimum Dwelling* were all filled with lush illustrations of stark, stunning, and on occasion even built modernist monuments in this vast Eurasian space. Antipodes like Teige and the 'encyclopaedian' Sigfried Giedion used the term *Constructivism* as a synonym for their version of Modernism.[82] The rise of Hitler led to most of Germany's leading Modernists literally upping sticks and moving to Moscow, and Mart Stam, Ernst May, Andre Lurçat, Hannes Meyer, Margarethe Schütte-Lihotsky and Bruno Taut were all living in the USSR by 1933, while Le Corbusier and Erich Mendelsohn had made visits and had their buildings constructed. Even Albert Kahn, 'Ford's Architect' was active there, though no doubt for less idealistic reasons.

So the obscurity of Soviet Modernism is a purely retrospective phenomenon. It's a delightful irony that the New York exhibition of Pare's photographs is at New York's Museum of Modern Art, as their defining *International Style* book/exhibition of 1932 was the first and most successful attempt to write this movement out of Modernist history. Philip Johnson (a man not known for his socialist sympathies) and Henry-Russell Hitchcock threw patrician scorn on 'fanatical functionalists' who would build for 'some proletarian superman of the future'[83], and included only one Soviet structure in their pinched, mean-spirited selection of white boxes. MOMA director Alfred H Barr had made trips to the USSR and been impressed by its Modernists: they *knew* this work existed, and deliberately excised it in order to present a Modernism less threatening to capitalist Amerika. After the turn to eclectic monumentalism imposed by Stalinist diktat in 1933-4, they would be aided in this by the Soviets themselves, who appeared to be utterly ashamed of their own experiments.

Post-war, even Johnson/Hitchcock's cursory references were absent: a typical history such as JM Richards' *Modern Architecture* (1953) features an impressive catalogue of interwar international modernists' names, and mentions one Soviet 'architect': Kasimir Malevich, whose designs never advanced further than plaster models.[84] Most histories of Modernism, in particular the rash of publications in the last 4 years, are quite comfortable about ignoring or dismissing the Soviet experiments.[85] A few drawings or models might make it in: Tatlin's tower, the Vesnin brothers' *Pravda* building with its glazed lifts, maybe Melnikov's built house and clubs, but always far outnumbered by the reassuring Western structures which have been lovingly restored over the last 20 years. So, via Pare's journey through the ruins, it's time to take a close look at what exactly *was* built, the ruins and wrecks and occasional well-kept up remnants left by the 'visitors' that pervade the former USSR, and then take another view of those wildly ambitious unbuilt, unbuildable utopian projects that, to misquote El Lissitzky, suggested an architecture for interstellar revolution.

The Revolution of Everyday Life

> *'A planetarium appeared in Moscow.*
> *This was an enormous fantastical apparatus. It was the – reali-*
> *sation of his fantasy.*
> *Made of black metal and glass.*
> *With forms that resembled no living creature.*
> *It was called the 'Martian'.*
> *It made him continue to search and search for a fantastical reality.*
> *Or for the fantasy in reality.'*
> Alexander Rodchenko, *Black and White - Autobiography*[86]

In 1929, the Moscow Planetarium, designed by the Constructivists Barsch & Sinyavsky, was completed. This was intended as a temple to popular science, offering visible proof to atheism and demonstrating the wonders of the Cosmos – a Planetarium had never been so politically loaded. In the late 30s, Rodchenko, confused and disappointed by Stalinism, recalled his pride at photographing this cosmic complex. The Planetarium survived Stalin and the anti-scientific lunacy of Lysenkoism, lived out the loss of the space race and survived the neoliberal chaos of the 1990s, then finally fell last year to Moscow's Mayor Yuri Luzhkov. The Moscow Architecture Preservation Society's detailed, dispiriting report *Moscow Heritage at Crisis Point* lists it as a 'lost' building: its glazed external staircase removed, its dome arbitrarily raised, its interior gutted.[87] As if to make totally clear that this was a victory for the Restoration, Luzhkov had an Orthodox Priest bless this 'reconstruction': an attempt at the interstellar quotidian was finally defeated.

Today, the aesthetics of everyday life are provided by speculative builders like Barratt Homes or Bellway, and the aesthetics of Capital by erstwhile avant-gardists, from Rogers and Foster to Koolhaas and Hadid[88]. The remarkable thing about Constructivism, something that can still be seen as a shadow, is that the everyday was the area for experiment. A much-used Russian term here was *Byt*, translated usually as Everyday Life, specifically in its most habituated, domestic sense. So most of the projects here were applications of the aesthetic that would be branded 'alien' by the Stalinists to the most basic architectural elements of society. That is, housing, public leisure facilities, schools, industrial areas integrated into the city, and local 'houses of the Soviet'.

Superficially, these buildings might seem similar to corresponding Western models: social housing, 'working men's clubs' and so forth, which we are used to thinking of as bastions of working-class conservatism. This was precisely why they were seen as so important, so it's the differences that are especially key here. This was frequently a *teleological* architecture, even a

Pavlovian one: particular social affects were intended to be produced. Although a socialist state power of some sort was claimed (rightly or wrongly) to be in place by 1922, its leaders were well aware that old habitus died hard: religion, patriarchy and 'petit bourgeois' attitudes still pervaded. In 1924, Leon Trotsky, a few years before his expulsion, published a book called *Problems of Everyday Life*. Here there was a cautious endorsement of 'Byt reform' – the experiments in living carried out at the time by communes and co-operatives – and the particular material forms that might house them. 'Public laundries, public restaurants, public workshops' would take the place of all that used to take place in the kitchen, thus abolishing 'household slavery'.[89] A poster from around this time shows a dingy, cramped kitchen being opened up to a glittering, glassy new world of futuristic structures and open space, and this was what was tentatively being constructed.

The Constructivist group OSA (Organisation of Contemporary Architects) had a phrase, 'the social condenser' to sum up the particular effects and processes that their architecture was intended to induce.[90] The Narkomfin Building, designed by Moisei Ginzburg and Ignati Milinis in 1928 for employees of the Commissariat of Finance, is the most famous and conspicuous of these buildings for a new *Byt*. Unlike most of the other ruins, there is an active campaign to save its remains. What we have here is a long, ribbon-windowed block, connected by a covered bridge to a glazed collective compound. The structure was designed to induce collectivism in its inhabitants: the duplex flats were divided into K-Types, which still provided space for children and cooking, and the F-Types that were 'fully collectivised', assuming that the children would be brought up in the collective block and the tenants would eat in the adjoining restaurant. The glazed block would feature all the facilities denied from the individual flats. Yet almost as soon as it was finished, the Narkomfin was denounced a remnant of 'leftist' utopianism, the pathos of one of

Charles Fourier's phalansteries somehow cut adrift in Stalinism.[91] A fate equally melancholic met the 'fully collectivised' *Dom Kommuna* designed by Ivan Nikolaev for the Textile Institute around the same time, which seems to be not so much crumbling as wilting.[92] If the Workers' Clubs are strange booze-free mutations of the WMC, then the Narkomfin has a similar relation to the luxury flats of today. Built, essentially, for bureaucrats, with duplexes and communal facilities, this is a prototype for every Ballardian Docklands block with its roof gardens, services and sexual experimentalism. Of course the Commissar, the old Bolshevik and part-time architect Nikolai Miliutin, occupied the penthouse.

Yet the Narkomfin and the Nikolaev Dom Kommuna were some of the first products of an intended standard for the whole of Russia, irrespective of status, domicile or class. Ginzburg, along with 3 other architects from the OSA Group, was employed by the state to develop typologies known as the Stroikom units. The F-Type and K-Type flats were pioneered here, as well as the adjoining public facilities: the high ceilings and duplexes were considered usable as a general standard for all, as opposed to a chic luxury. The rise of Stalin and the accompanying mass indus-trialisation actually killed off this exercise in Standardisation rather than encouraging it, and only 6 complexes applying these principles were ever built (which still beats the amount of Unités d'Habitation Le Corbusier managed to get built 20-30 years later, borrowing many Stroikom ideas). *The Lost Vanguard* features one of the others, by Ginzburg and Alexander Pasternak, in Ekaterinburg. In rather better condition than the Narkomfin, its alternation of glazed strips, curves and sharp angles still looks like a viable, if ghostly, standard. The curious pink hue reminds that the white box International Style that archive photos give these buildings was often an illusion. The OSA architects were great enthusiasts for bright, artificial chromaticism: a whole issue of their journal, *SA* was devoted to the question, and the Bauhaus' colour expert Hinnerk Scheper was in the USSR at the time collaborating on their projects.

The Platonic white still got a few applications, appealing in its ability to sweep away the clutter and waste of the past. An anecdote in a contemporary women's magazine featured a tenant using a whitewash gun in a new Dom Kommuna 'because it shoots the old *Byt* dead!'[93] Other, less ambitious housing blocks are scattered across the former USSR, rather less dogmatic in design than 'classical' Modernism: strange motifs abound, such as the half-arches of Nikolsky/Gegello/Simonov's Tractor Street flats in St Petersburg, or the jaggedness of a doctors' co-op in Kiev. Occasionally the lightness and airiness is replaced with something more imposing and sinister, such as in Boris Iofan's bombastic Constructivist-Classical House on the Embankment in Moscow, later known as the 'house of ghosts' for the amount of old Bolshevik residents who were purged.

Then there are the public buildings: the factory kitchens and workers' clubs. Most wildly impressive are the three collective kitchens designed by ASNOVA architects for St Petersburg. ASNOVA was the most 'formalist' of the avant-garde groups, and their past of designing floating restaurants and skyscrapers has more than a trace here. One of them, as mentioned above, is now a thoroughly picked carcass in Pare's photographs: you can make out that the new world was built partly in wood. The Workers' Clubs were a Bolshevik pet project, intended to provide, as Trotsky put it in 1924, a 'bridge' between the old world and the new: 'leading out of the close little cage of the family flat with its ikons and image lamp' into socialist citizenship and culture.[94] You can see these places in films like Dziga Vertov's *Man with a Movie Camera*: converted churches, housing libraries and games rooms. However the most famous were the new-build projects of the Trade Unions, which had a precarious independence – Konstantin Melnikov's series of clubs in Moscow were all for the unions, and repudiated standardisation in favour of individual works of art, with the most famous of them, the Rusakov Club (one of the handful of Constructivist buildings that has some sort of international fame) a still astonishing conflict of tension and force – 'a volley aimed at the future' as he called it himself.[95]

El Lissitzky, at one time an ASNOVA member, wrote that the clubs would not be places where people passively consumed entertainment: 'the important thing is that the mass of the members must be directly involved. They themselves must find in it the maximum of self-expression.'[96] The architecture was intended by some to help inspire this expression, as perhaps in Melnikov's clubs or in Ilya Golosov's justly famous Zuev Club, while the OSA social condensers, like the Vesnin brothers' labyrinthine Palace of Culture of the Likachev Works (on the site of a demolished monastery) had more directly *byt*-transformative intent: its internal volumes have been compared to Wright's Guggenheim, similarly announcing the immediate existence of a new world.[97] The Likachev Club has its own observatory, so the workers in the nearby car factory could have a link with the stars, even if they couldn't have a drink.

The most breathtaking of all Constructivist projects has to be

Richard Pare, Vasilievsky Factory Kitchen

the Gosprom Complex (or 'Palace of Industry') in the Ukrainian city of Kharkov. There can't have been anything else of this scale and ambition anywhere else in Europe at the time: indeed, it resembles more some particularly ambitious work of the late 1960s than the mid-20s, an unacknowledged prototype of that 60s motif, the elevated walkway, the street in the sky. Constructed between 1926 and 1928, apparently by volunteers from the local Komsomol, this is *Metropolis* – or *Aelita* – actualised. Concrete and glass blocks from 7 to 13 storeys connected by skyways, curving round a huge public square, this resembles a small city in its own right. Its designers, Serafimov, Kravets and Felger, appear to have been as obscure at the time as they have been since, yet only an El Lissitsky, a Gropius or a Corbusier were designing anything as ambitious in 1926. Eisenstein and Vertov both used it on film (*The General Line* and *Three Songs of Lenin*, respectively), aptly, as the contrasts, angles and multiple levels had spatial affinities to their montage techniques: more literally, Friedrich Ermler used it in *Fragment of Empire*, a Communist Rip van Winkle tale, as exemplar of the incomprehensible new world that the sleeper awakes to.

There are innumerable other fragments and interventions in *The Lost Vanguard*, too many to list here, their degeneration too extensive to itemise. A few scattered masterpieces worth mentioning: a water tower in Ekaterinburg proudly atop a post-industrial waste; a Ballardian photograph of a diving board in Kiev looking down into a drained pool; a series of clubs, kitchens, flats and the elegant hammer & sickle topped Kirov District Soviet in Narvskaya Zastava[98], St Petersburg; great lost and forlorn buildings by Corbusier and Mendelsohn…If there was an orthodoxy here, then it's a style of long fenestration bands broken by graceful curves (according to the theorist Mikhail Okhitovich, the right-angle was a remnant of the capitalist allocation of land) akin to a more futuristic and generous International Style, and this can be seen from Baku to Ivanovo. Most gorgeously, in Sochi on

Richard Pare, Narvskaya Factory Kitchen

the Black Sea, with three sanatorium complexes preceding and
rivalling Aalto's breakthrough at Paimio. One of these, by the
Vesnin brothers, recently became a base for soldiers serving in the
dirty war in Chechnya. Van Damme posters rather than revolutionary exhortations adorn the walls. This reminder of macho,
Putinite state brutality is by no means an exclusively contemporary phenomenon. Some of these buildings housed the courts
and police offices that would sentence countless innocents to
their deaths in the later 30s, while a fair few social condensers

were designed for 'Chekists': secret policemen, members of the NKVD, whose socialist morality was presumably in need of encouragement from the architecture.

The Chekists' Housing Project in Ekaterinburg contains a remarkable spiralling staircase, an inexorable passage upwards. In fact, perhaps the most original feature of most of the buildings here seems to have been their stairwells and ramps, the mark of what Lewis Mumford would no doubt have considered a 'sun-worshipping' culture. All of them seem to curve, cantilever and vault upwards as if aiming, in Malevich & Kruchenykh's phrase, for 'Victory over the Sun'. Even the most modest, sober structures sheath some kind of interstellar passageway. Pare's photos here seem consciously to pay tribute to the original photographic explorers of these thrusting spaces: a shot of Nikolaev's Textile Institute's geometric stairs references Boris Ignatovich, while the internal ramps at Corbusier's Centrosoyus make his abstract theories of 'circulation' seem a stunningly fluid reality. This is an architecture of perpetual motion, which makes it especially poignant that it was so quickly brought to a halt.

The Institute for the Transformation of Mankind

'No matter what happens, we must avoid being strangled by the dead past'.
Nikolai Miliutin, *Sotsgorod* (1930)[99]

Modernism was always an element of Bolshevik modernity, irrespective of the personal tastes of its leaders, and a Modernist city is promised in the posters and propaganda of the 1920s and early 1930s. In fact, this was perhaps the first, maybe only time that Modernist architecture was directly used as an instrument of state propaganda. Posters depicted built structures like the *Izvestia* headquarters or the Rodchenko-decorated Mosselprom store, or created architectural fantasies of skyscraper cities, communal kitchens or Corbusian workers' towns. Then there's the nervous, sexy city that features in the film posters of the Stenberg brothers, with their romantic and sinister fictionalised America. The fellow traveller literature of the earlier 30s always featured grainy shots of clean-lined workers' dwellings, clubs, and houses of the Soviet.[100] This is what Soviet socialism was originally supposed to look like, a promise made and reneged upon. Imagine if it hadn't been, that the paragon of the Twentieth Century's inorganic desires was a Delirious Moscow rather than New York.[101]

Then you come up against a block. Unavoidable in any discussion of this architecture is just how short-lived it all was. Although the time period here is '22-32', most comes from after 1927, the period in which Stalin began picking off his opponents, first on the internationalist Left, then on the humanitarian Right, then launching a murderous collectivisation in the countryside and massive industrialisation. There was brief encouragement in a short-lived 'cultural revolution' that accompanied the first Five Year Plan, but by the time they were finished, most of these buildings were already antique, associated with a 'Trotskyist' or 'bohemian' or literally 'alien' approach[102]: hence, they never had the opportunity to be truly lived-in, never became accepted by the population at large. After once being a wing of state propaganda, they became an embarrassment, frequently refaced with stone and neoclassical ornament. This, nearly almost as much as Cold War politics, helps explain their obscurity, but so, perhaps, does the huge amount of paper architecture in the period. Best to think about the untainted, ahistorical utopian blueprint than the actual constructed reality.

For all that, no paper architecture had been this exciting, or would be again for decades, and no discussion of the period is complete without it. This, though, is where the alienation effect lessens somewhat: anyone interested in 20th century architecture has seen an image of Tatlin's tower, and its familiarity enables it to be slotted into a series of clichés about utopian dreams or the oh-so-poignant hopefulness of the revolution before it starts to devour its children. Nonetheless, let's leave reality behind for a bit and return to the productions of Red Planet Mars. J Hoberman described *Aelita* as 'an innocently Trotskyist fantasy of interplanetary solidarity'[103], and maybe the best book to document the paper projects is El Lissitzky's *Russland*, written in German in 1929: quite in contrast to the Stalinist policy of nationalism and secrecy, this was an internationalist tract, showing the Soviet examples as exemplars of what a revolutionary architecture could be like *everywhere*.

Some of the most daring projects here came out of the ASNOVA group, who had already attracted international attention, perhaps in part because their work seemed to be designed for technologies far beyond Russian capabilities. Nikolai Ladovsky's workshop at the Vkhutemas school harnessed a 'psycho-technical method' to an explosive interpretation of the skyscraper vocabulary and to some peculiar restaurants and hotels, hanging from peaks or descending down slopes: Zaha Hadid's The Peak (1981) took obvious tips from these designs. El Lissitzky's own horizontal skyscrapers for Moscow, the *Wolkenbügel* (skyhook), have a similar afterlife: Koolhaas' CCTV building in part seems a wilfully irregular use of the same idea. The student projects from Vkhutemas are like a meeting point between the Neues Bauen and Buckminster Fuller: take Ivan Leonidov's Lenin Institute, a glass ball suspended from a tower full of books. His town-planning projects and unbuilt clubs, long a touchstone for Deconstructivists, have been related to Malevich's Suprematist painting: accordingly, Malevich's own 'buildings' are in Lissitzky's book, three dimensional interstellar architecture ('planits') made up of squares and rectangles, taking the stepping of New York skyscrapers out of the zoning code and into the future...much of this was literally science fictional, as some basic Western building techniques were rare in the USSR. A skyscraper was almost as improbable in 1923 as Kriutikov's Flying City would be 5 years later. This ASNOVA scheme merely takes literally a SF socialism implicit in the more seemingly buildable projects.

Curves and cylinders were, as in the built projects, constant motifs, only here with even more explicit interplanetary content. Alexander Nikolsky's bathhouse for St Petersburg, a retractable glass dome that would be pricey to build even today is one extreme example, as are what appear to be extraterrestrial *siedlungen* by one Kotschar at the Vkhutemas school: a few row houses straight out of the Neue Frankfurt catalogue aligned with towering rotundas. Similarly, Lissitzky's book has an office complex by Siltschenko, another student, made up of the same – again, more 60s than 20s in immediate appearance, akin somewhat to the Capitol records tower in fact – arranged into a ringed square. Not in Lissitzky, but equally spaceage was a design for a headquarters for the Communist International by Lydia Komarova, made up of spiralling glass cylinders: politically as well as technically this was dangerously utopian, as World Revolution was decisively off the agenda under Stalin. However it was partly because of Lissitzky's book that the Neues Bauen transferred itself eastwards en bloc – they'd expected the new world to be already awaiting them, rather than fighting a rearguard action against medieval technics and a philistine bureaucracy. One flaw of *The Lost Vanguard* is that it doesn't go to the new towns planned by Ernst May (Magnitogorsk and many others), or offer any insight into what, if anything, ever actually got built by Taut, Meyer's 'Bauhaus Brigade' et al in their Moscow years.[104] Perhaps there's nothing left. May, after all, claimed that he was lucky to escape with his life when he and the other German 'specialists' were hounded out in the mid-30s.

The other key book for the migrants was *Sotsgorod* ('Socialist City') a proposal for linear cities by Commissar Nikolai Miliutin, occupant of the Narkomfin penthouse: and the post-war new towns in the West can trace themselves back to the likes of Magnitogorsk, disavowed though that might be. The controversy over the socialist city broke out in 1930 over the 'Green City' competition for a sort of spa town outside of Moscow. Melnikov's proposal was taken as a satirical jibe, a city of sleep for a country descending into coercion and surveillance and with ever-increasing working hours. Sweetly, he wrote: 'while undertaking to expand the scope of architecture, I surprised myself and will surprise all of you by my arithmetic: one third of life is spent lying without consciousness, without any guide in the mysterious world of sleep, and tapping the unseen depth of the source of healing secrets...well, this may be the miracle of miracles, indeed anything can be a miracle.'[105] The inhabitants' sleep would be subliminally affected by smells, sounds and spatiality so that even in dreaming they were reachable by the authorities; yet Melnikov seemed breezily naïve about his proposal, and at the centre of it he placed an 'institute for the transformation of mankind'. Still, a phrase like 'and what's more, the whole world has fallen asleep' in his accompanying explanation seemed dangerously ambiguous.

The contest here highlighted two competing town planning ideas among the avant-garde. The first was 'urbanism', led by one Leonid Sabsovich. Despite the name, this was basically a version of the garden city on a massive scale, with huge collective blocks dispersed across the countryside. Extending the 'social condenser' idea to whole cities, this was a particularly utopian kind of urbanism, in which marriage and property would be obliterated at one stroke, an architectural Sexpol in which 'divorces' were achieved by the moving of a partition. But more important for Western Modernists, especially in the CIAM, were the proposals for disurbanism. The sociologist Mikhail Okhitovich had converted Moisei Ginzburg, a member of the CIAM's central committee, and most of the OSA Group, to a radically dispersed notion of city planning. This was a response to a situation in which the city and country were virtually at civil war, and huge primitive accumulation led to cities acquiring favela-like makeshift outskirts. Instead of designing new cities or expanding the old, Okhitovich wanted them exploded into vast networks connected by advanced transportation networks, stretching all the way across the countryside. In the current situation of explosive 'informal' cities without infrastructure springing up worldwide, this could be considered a theory of cities designed for their inhabitants to use and discard at will, as much as an inadvertent prophecy of Los Angeles.

That isn't a facetious comparison. Like the Smithsons, who claimed that the problem with modern homes was that they weren't as well designed as caravans, Okhitovich admired mobile homes, and the freewheeling approach to putting down one's (temporary) roots. A Hollywood film like Buster Keaton's *One Week* (1920), where the prefabricated house skids down the street, is as much a component of disurbanism as the pieties of the Garden city. Okhitovich's 'Theory of Resettlement' is reminiscent of the Bolshevik preference for merging revolution and speed in a very literal sense: as in Trotsky's Civil War train with its library and printing press, the famed agit-trains, or Alexander Medvedkin's travelling film-studio.[106] Maybe even a suppressed memory of Nestor Makhno's Anarchist 'Republic on Wheels'[107]. 'The house of the future (will be) a standardised, motorised, easily transportable, small and hence inexpensive structure', was the claim.[108] This isn't just an Autopia, but explicitly an attempt to merge the city and country, preserving the live aspects of both, rather than obliterating the village for the metropolis. It is that paradoxical thing, 'organic Constructivism'.[109]

While the International Style planning approach, with its zoning and edifices, was purist and Platonic, disurbanist theory was based on fluidity and changeability. In the OSA group journal *Sovremennaia Arkitektura* Alexander Pasternak wrote that the fixed house was an 'anachronism, apathetic and out of place, no longer an active participant in an active and fast moving life'.[110] The houses being developed by the OSA at this time were prefabricated, both easy for people to assemble and dismantle, and were intended to be provided by the state to individuals who could do whatever they liked with them: Moisei Ginzburg's prototypes could additively make two linked houses, or be put together to make a communal block if the inhabitants so wished.[111] *SA* declared that the notion of a building built to last was henceforth over. Another prototype, based on a Vkhutemas diploma project by Sokolov consisted of cylindrical pods placed in untamed

Konstantin Melnikov, Svodboda Workers Club

countryside. There was here an extreme of collectivism, with a total abolition of private property and extension of communal facilities, and at the same time an extreme of individualism, with each person having their own single dwelling, whether male or female, in a couple or not: a 'pod of one's own', as it were. The plan of these settlements was in the form of interlinked ribbons, each one representing a strip of industry, agriculture, transport, cultural facilities and housing.

When these proposals were put across at the Green City exhibition in 1930, Le Corbusier, soon to be made by *The International Style* into the model for all to follow, was asked to give his views on the projects: this would become the *Response to Moscow*, more famous as *The Radiant City*. The final form of this book dwells often on the follies of Soviet disurbanism. Private letters between himself and Moisei Ginzburg from 1930 showed that this was a debate in which Corbusier was the collectiviser and the Soviet architect the individualist, even though Ginzburg

Gustav Klutsis, 'To live culturally is to work productively'

wrote that 'you want to cure the city, because you are trying to keep it essentially the same as capitalism made it'.[112] While the *Response to Moscow* eulogised the Plan, seeing it as a despotic force, a Napoleonic 'tribune of the people'[113], the Soviet disurbanists eulogised a kind of democratic planning in the tradition of council communism. When the collective networks of industry and transport were provided and property was eliminated, then people could live wherever they decided to put their pod. Okhitovich claimed that that 'the stronger the collective links, the stronger the individual personality'.[114] This is a conception far from the familiar opposition of on one side the fixed, monolithic plan, as in the CIAM's postwar outgrowths, and on the other the capitalist anarchy of leaving the free market to remake the city in its image. At the same time it suggests an approach to the divide between city and country that has been resolutely untried, despite the aforementioned superficial similarities with the Californian approach to urban cohesiveness.

This is mainly because history would soon catch up these experiments. A CIAM conference was planned to be held in Moscow in 1933. However the notorious Palace of the Soviets

competition of that year showed the direction that the rise of Stalinism was taking architecture and planning – a huge, monumental city centrepiece, although most CIAM architects took part anyway: Corbusier's entry, with its vast Constructivist arch, became the source of later designs by Oscar Niemeyer and Norman Foster.[115] But to concentrate on the Capital was the opposite of the OSA's suggestions. Okhitovich and Ginzburg had advocated demolishing much of Moscow, which would revert to a giant park filled with monuments. Yet here was the capital stamping its authority on the country: the 'cult of hierarchy' that Okhitovich had explicitly criticised.[116] The CIAM did have one small conference in Moscow in December 1932, with CIAM general secretary Sigfried Giedion and others meeting Ginzburg and the OSA group, yet the game was obviously up: the winner of the Palace of the Soviets competition was a huge neoclassical edifice by Boris Iofan, designer of the House of the Embankment that looks so intimidating in Pare's photographs. Giedion actually sent a telegram and a photomontage in protest to Stalin, which, fortunately for him, was never received. In a letter to Corbusier, Giedion outlined the contradictions of the CIAM's position: opposed to untrammelled capitalism, yet forced to suppress their politics in order to get work. He asked: 'should we be technicians or politicians?' If the latter, it would be 'impossible to have an influence with anyone important at the moment', especially after the rise of Hitler cut off the other centre of Modernism.[117]

And at this point, the conjuncture in which Socialist

Andrei Burov, set for Eisenstein's The General Line

68

Cities were the fixation of Modern architects as much as Dubai skyscrapers are for their contemporary descendants was finished. Yet in 1933 was published one of the great last hurrahs of Constructivism, and a return to the science fiction from which it emerged: Iakov Chernikhov's book

Gosprom, Kharkov, as used in The General Line

Architectural Fantasies. The designer was prolific in industry, (at least one factory building survives in St Petersburg) yet was by no means a participant in any of the period's major debates. This perhaps helps leave his plans untainted by history and by the ruination that has overtaken his contemporaries. Accordingly, these images, crackling with electricity, depict a garish industrial utopia resembling space stations more than earthbound Dom Kommuny. The images are archetypal Futurism: pervaded by a rhythmic, shuddering awe and anticipation at an onrushing new world. Chernikhov wrote of the fantasies as revealing the 'hidden desires' of the architect.[118]

Soon to be hidden because suppressed, of course. Nevertheless, Chernikhov's books became a sort of image bank for high-tech architects in the 1980s, revealing that their employment does not in itself cause the world to be transfigured. When the 'alien building' is a bank or an office block it can become an object of distant, awed contemplation. When, on the other hand, the alien enters everyday life, when it can't be ignored but has to be lived with, then the boundaries between the alien nation and our alienated cities might start to be breached.

3: Revolutionary Orgasm Problems

Sexpol – the Sexual Economy of Marxist Modernism

'When the body has completely become an object, a beautiful thing, it can foreshadow a new happiness. In suffering the most extreme reification man triumphs over reification'
Herbert Marcuse, 'The Affirmative Character of Culture' (1937)[119]

'I still dream of Orgonon...I wake up crying'
Kate Bush, 'Cloudbusting' (1985)[120]

What happens to the libidinal imaginary when mystique, mystery, myth, and the stage sets of the Romantic are stripped away? What happens when we propose a love and a sexuality without camouflage, and try to propose alternatives to the profoundly depressing notion that one can only fall in love in buildings of the 18th century, and try, instead, to imagine love in the Collective blocks? Herbert Marcuse's 1937 essay imagines a realisation of such aesthetically loaded terms as beauty and love, via an elimination of their mystical character, the force which immediately gives the patina of 'romanticism' to stern exercises in Imperial neo-classicism like the National Gallery or the bombastic boulevards of Paris. This still forms our mental catalogue of all things romantic, with love and desire transliterated into curlicues and Corinthian columns. In a 2006 piece for one of the broadsheet *Modernism* supplements, J.G Ballard wrote of his 'regret' that no-one could fall in love in the Heathrow Hilton, while 'people were falling in love in the Louvre all the time...[121] For Marcuse, to leave the argument at that, or as Socialist Realists advocated, take up bourgeois culture columns and all for the proletariat, or reproduce its values in a new style, led both avant-gardists and

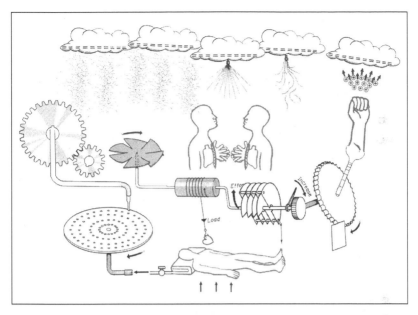

Lydia Thompson, 'Love Operation'

leftist aesthetic traditionalists to 'miss the main point: the abolition of this culture'.[122] This is what made leftist Modernisms so harsh: the need to assert a counter, to create another culture, something the left is at present utterly unwilling to do, endlessly harping on about 'resistance', without the slightest notion of victory, let alone what culture should exist afterwards.

'Sexpol', as an appropriately Bolshevik acronym, derives from the 1930s work of renegade Freudian Wilhelm Reich, in books like *The Sexual Revolution, The Invasion of Compulsory Sex-Morality* and the pamphlet written for the Kommunistische Partei Deutschlands, *Dialectical Materialism and Psychoanalysis*. Reich's own Berlin practice tried to extend psychoanalysis from the bourgeois couch to the proletarian city-block, yet his works advocate many ideas which have since become wholly, boringly acceptable – the release from the alleged repressions and prohibitions on sexuality that marked bourgeois society. And the decline in birth rates, marriages and the acceptability of the genital prose-

71

lytised here have all become normal features of European late capitalism. However to regard this as a won battle is to ignore Reich's most central point, namely that the freedom from sexual oppression is meaningless without freedom from economic, i.e. that sexual freedom is a condition of Communism and vice versa.

Rather than being dismissed as cranky, his ideas had currency in the Weimar Republic's Communist movement, as can be seen in the none more *sachlich* treatment of sexual matters in films like *Kuhle Wampe* or the KPD's campaigns for abortion on demand. The KPD even distributed a Reich-authored sex education book aimed at 8 to 12 year olds, *The Sexual Struggle of Youth*. And this tendency is not reducible to the proper name 'Reich', which is a little unhelpful given his, shall we say, eccentric later theories – of equal importance were Magnus Hirschfeld's Berlin Institute

of Sexology, dedicated to the overturning of sexual divisions in the name of socialism, or the writings and campaigns of Alexandra Kollontai for sexual equality and against an incipient Puritanism in the USSR. Sexpol makes a return in the 1960s,

Still from Abram Room's Bed and Sofa

the other 20th century moment when a counter-cultural avant-garde, socialist politics and demands for sexual revolution met. Some revolutionaries have avoided this as a question altogether: Rosa Luxemburg once rather cutely compared discussions of sexual politics to the pseudo-revolutionary posing of Reformists: one should *do it* rather than talk about it.[123] But nonetheless: here's some talk.

Energetic Functionalism

> *'The Oedipus complex is a socially conditioned fact which changes its form with the structure of society. The Oedipus complex must disappear in a socialist society, because its social basis, the patriarchal family, will itself disappear, having lost its raison d'etre. Communal upbringings, which form part of the socialist programme, will be so unfavourable to the forming of social attitudes as they exist within the family today – the relationship of children to one another and to the persons who bring them up will be so much more many-sided, complex and dynamic – that the Oedipus complex with its specific content of desiring the mother and wishing to destroy the father will lose its meaning.'*[124]

Wilhelm Reich, *Dialectical Materialism and Psychoanalysis* (1929)

Isn't it the case, though, that that the increasingly industrialist, functionalist bent of the modernist avant-garde left out the dream life of the 20th century, that Freud had to be repressed in order to apotheosize Lenin? The exceptions to this, the attempts to close the divide between sexualised surrealism and ascetic Constructivism, can actually be found in the avowedly Communist architectural theory that was forcibly expelled from mainstream Modernism as it became canonical in the 1930s. The CIAM mainstream gradually expunged these elements, so Modernism as it spread worldwide was always missing them. But for that, Le Corbusier had his own take on the sex appeal of reinforced concrete. During the 1930s his Purist pilotis began quite deliberately taking on the form of a particularly formidable woman's thigh, his paintings frequently dwelling on the steatopygous: allegedly he once tried to hit on a journalist with the line 'you are fat, and I like my women fat'.[125] The myth is that while Corbusier was opened up to sensualism, the protagonists of

73

the minimum-wohnung, whether the Germans who headed East rather than West to escape the rise of Nazism, or the Soviets, insisted on a dry, sexless Functionalism. Yet what Reich eventually decided upon as a name for his psychoanalytic theory was 'Energetic Functionalism' – and the 1929 pamphlet that Reich wrote specifically for the KPD, *Dialectical Materialism and Psychoanalysis*, posits a collective cure as much as the talking one.

Le Corbusier, meanwhile, was actually quite sympathetic to Soviet Constructivism, which he (rather insightfully) saw as 'the vehicle of an intensely lyrical intent, one that is even potentially transcendent...a poetic idea'.[126] The body of Constructivist architectural theory could in fact be perceived as a kind of architectural Sexpol. The Urbanist Leonid Sabsovich, who imagined the new society organised as serial Dom Kommuny (house-collectives, not to be confused with the Kommunalka, which were pre-revolutionary dwellings subdivided and usually grossly overcrowded), considered this to open up the possibilities of new forms of sexual relations. Marriage and property would be obliterated, for rooms of one's own for men and women, irrespective of marital status: as he put it, everyone in the dom-kommuna was a potential 'bachelor', 'husband' or 'wife', 'to the extent that today's bachelor may be tomorrow's husband and today's couple may tomorrow be separated': 'divorces' could be achieved by the sliding of the partition-like walls.[127] Alongside Bolsheviks like Kollontai or poets such as Vladimir Mayakovsky (whose ménage a trois with Lili and Osip Brik was very public) they suspected that a masculine revolutionary politics avoided the question of Byt – the Russian word meaning everyday life, with particular stress on its most banal, conservative aspects – and that Byt would be the new battleground.

Although this speaks of a liberation from previous models of sexuality, it can often become a rather regimented, Taylorist kind of sex-economy. In this the Constructivists evoke Zamyatin's highly ambiguous novel *We*, wherein the sexual ethic of the One-

Moisei Ginzburg & Ignati Milinis, Narkomfin building

State is similarly based on pleasure, rationalism and regimentation. The blinds in the glass communal houses can be lowered for the 'sexual hours', anyone can be chosen as a partner provided of course that our lovers first fill in the attendant pink coupon. Here a sexual liberation of a sort has been achieved, yet without any ostentatious display, without an attendant sexualisation and vulgarisation of society as a whole. Sexual energies may still be sublimated, powering the One State's technological marvels, but we are miles from either Orwell's anti-sex league or Huxley's repressive desublimation. Children, naturally, are raised collectively. This was achieved, albeit briefly, in the architectural experiments with Soviet sex-economy. Two Moscow apartment blocks were examples of this: Moisei Ginzburg's 'semi-collectivised' Narkomfin Building eliminated individual kitchens, added crèches and a library as part of the housing complex and attempted to discourage the privatisation of marital relations, while the Textile Institute block designed by Ivan Nikolaev forbade the student inhabitants to spend time in their 'cabins for living' during the day, lest they develop a bourgeois conception of their own personal hearth. The building was strictly divided into areas sanitary, dormitory and daytime, yet if this all sounds rather severe, such collective houses were clamped down upon by the Stalin clique partly because of their rather loose sexual morality.

One that impressed Reich, who wrote, in *The Invasion of Compulsory Sex-Morality* (1931) of this peculiar pragmatic utopianism; 'the moral atmosphere seemed, at first, ascetic: no sexual importuning in the street; reserve and seriousness everywhere...at social gatherings the absence of the sexual allusions and smutty conversation characteristic of our circles. If a man dared slap a woman's backside he might well be prosecuted before the party tribunal. But the question whether one wanted to become a sexual partner was being asked more and more openly and unhesitatingly: sexual companionship without any underhandedness, women's genitality a matter of course.'[128] What seems utopian about both what Reich describes and what Zamyatin rather mischievously elucidates, is the possibility of sexual freedom without an attendant hypersexualisation, a direct inverse of a the puritan prurience of contemporary society. Reich saw a partial fulfilment of his idea that sexual irrationalism was directly correlative to the economic irrationalism of capital. He writes for instance of an acquaintance who was eight months pregnant, with no-one knowing or asking who the father was, or of two men in a commune agreeing to jointly support the child of a lover they both shared, as they didn't care to argue which was the father (this is similar to a scenario in the 1927 film *Bed and Sofa*). Reich claimed that he saw 'the economic outlines of a future sex hygiene of the masses in impressive efforts to raise all members of society to a high cultural level through higher wages and shorter working hours, as well as cultural mass education and a stand against religion.'[129] But by 1934 the psychoanalyst felt that he had to add a footnote to this, retracting his earlier praise of the USSR, whose reactionary turn he analysed in *The Sexual Revolution* a year later. The actual achievement of industrial and technological modernity through the Five Year Plans had coincided with a clampdown on this new sexual morality. Utopia abandoned at the point of its possible realisation.

Physical Culture in the Love Hotel and the Minimum Dwelling

> *Webster watched the images of the young woman on the screen, sections of her body intercut with pieces of modern architecture. All these buildings. What did Talbert want to do - sodomise the Festival Hall?*
> J.G Ballard, *The Atrocity Exhibition* (1969)[130]

Le Corbusier's anti-Romantic antagonists, the vociferous Czechoslovakian Functionalists such as architect Jiri Kroha and the editor, designer and propagandist Karel Teige, were responsible for some straightforwardly carnal works, usually employing photomontage. Kroha, for a book on 'Hygiene', created one collage of naked, male and female bodies, their pulchritude presented as an element of *Fizkultura* ('physical culture'), of a rational approach to the human body, free of romantic mystification – something that is totally undercut by qualities that Kroha himself had no control over. Namely that these men with their sharp hairstyles and wiry bodies, the women with flapper haircuts and very early 20th century generous proportions, and the sepia tone of the photographs, gives to them an inadvertent fetishistic eroticism – fashion defeating function.

A rather cleverer treatment of the line of the female body can be seen in Karel Teige's 'Alphabet' montages, where a woman in what could conceivably be a sports costume, a kind of *sachlich* undergarment or swimwear, contorts herself into a new system of physical language based on angular polarities, bodily exertion combined with anti-naturalism. One difference is that Teige's work deliberately deals with sexual *provocation*. It suggests that the human body will be able to do new things, that the dream-life of the machine for living in, the libido of the minimum dwelling, will have all manner of possibilities unencumbered by an

accepted idea of eroticism: the courting couples at the Louvre so defeatedly cited by Ballard in 2006 replaced by the post-Fordist erotic geometry of the Ballard of 1969 and his *Atrocity Exhibition*. The angle between two walls, the spark and friction of man-made surface.

Teige was an ardent defender of functionalism at it's most hard-line, his 1932 book *The Minimum Dwelling* being one of the most famous tracts advocating an extreme reductivism for a Communist Architecture. A line could actually be

Grigori Shegal, 'Down with Kitchen Slavery'

traced from Teige's micro-houses to the musical Microhouse of a 2000s Central European label like Perlon, which follows like Teige a combination of the mechanoid and the licentious by way of setting extreme limitations on itself; and a Ricardo Villalobos track, with its stripped, man-made pulsions, squelches and dry liquidity would surely be the perfect music for one of the flats advocated by Teige. In *The Minimum Dwelling* Teige keeps coming back to the limiting of personal space and the extension of public: one of the exemplars, for him, are the massive hotels of New York, enabling leisure outside of the 'living cell' – but this is done to eliminate what he calls 'sexual banality'.[131] The more minimal the dwelling, the more extensive the sexual imaginary, and, it was for this that the married couple were discouraged from sharing a room. Teige has some surprising comrades here. Andrea Dworkin quoted *The Sexual Revolution* when she wrote in *Intercourse* that

'Wilhelm Reich, that most optimistic of sexual liberationists, the only male one to abhor rape really, thought that a girl needed not only "a free genital sexuality" but also "an undisturbed room, proper contraceptives, a friend who is capable of love, that is, not a National Socialist . . . " All remain hard for women to attain; but especially the lover who is not a National Socialist'.[132]

So Teige's use of a particularly extreme form of Surrealist photomontage need not be seen as a retreat from his Functionalist preoccupations but a representation of their possible dream life: utopian, quotidian and dystopian. They also coincide with his public break with Stalinism, leaving the Party in 1937 and blasting it in the essay 'Surrealism Against the Current'. A few of Tiege's montages are dreamlike titillation, reorganisations of the human body into landscapes with no purpose other than polymorphous perversity, uncoincidentally cocking a snook at the Puritanism of the Stalinised USSR. Utopianism transferred to the body itself. Others make Sexpol puns reminiscent of the wry photoplastics of Moholy-Nagy, militarism juxtaposed with girlie mags juxtaposed with adverts. Where they become unnerving is when war makes incursions upon them, when their benignly diffuse bodies become forcibly diffused, when actual cruelty and destruction supplants the artistic. In a 2007 paper, Jennifer Hui Bon Hoa related Ballard's *Atrocity Exhibition* to Siegfried Kracauer's reading of the Tiller Girls, *The Mass Ornament*.[133] While Kracauer saw Ford sexually mimetised in the angles and repetitive movements of the dancers, *The Atrocity Exhibition* eroticised postwar fragmentation, its protagonist creating collages of pornography, advertising, medical diagrams and Modernist architecture to re-imagine sexuality. This sounds almost like a description of Teige's montages, and like Ballard's tortured Traven, these works are caught between new, undreamt of possibility and violent rupture.

The avant-garde of the 1980s would celebrate near impossible physical feats, Mapplethorpe's Lisa Lyon photos encapsulating an elite form of physical discipline, the 20s vanguard worked at the level of everyday life. Typical is a Marcel Breuer photo of a recumbent sportswoman, slightly dumpy but asymmetrically haired, sat by a record player with impeccable cool. Outside of the explicit provocations of Le Corbusier and Teige (in their very different ways) were the more accepted forms of confrontation with the non-machinic body. *Fizkultura* denoted the sports organisations and *Spartakiadas* which were an alternative to the classicist, capitalist Olympiads – how curious, given the Eastern Bloc's later obsession with Olympic record-breaking, down to forcible medical attempts to break down gender divisions in order to achieve it. These festivals of the Labour Movement became an obvious training ground for protagonists of the man-machine.

Still from Makavejev's Switchboard Operator

This can be seen in many of the greatest works of the cinematic montageurs of the 20s and early 30s, bodily leaps and feats reacting dialectically with their own chops and cuts – from the reverse diving boards of Vertov's *Kino-Eye* to the sports festival of *Kuhle Wampe*, all eagerly cannibalised by Riefenstahl. Or in the form of photo-montage, the riotous poster designs by Gustav Klutsis for the 1928 Spartakiada, tensions encoded in clashing colours and preposterous angles.

This merging of mass sport and mass politics makes us justifiably suspicious. There is another side to this, however: for instance, Le Corbusier's proposal in *The Radiant City* for the creation of a participatory physical culture suggests something quite unlike the spectacles of the rallies and Olympiads. The passage in Herbert Marcuse's essay in the *Zeitschrift für Sozialforschung* we began with talks about the forms of demotic more acceptable to the leftist intellectual, but is nonetheless apposite here: 'the artistry of the beautiful body, its effortless agility and relaxation, which can be displayed today only in the circus, vaudeville and burlesque, herald the joy to which will attain in being liberated to the ideal, in which man, having become a true subject, succeeds in the mastery of matter.'[134] This physical exuberance, when spread on a mass scale, has similarities with another Constructivist incursion into mass culture: the flapper dresses of Varvara Stepanova and Lyubov Popova, where the reification that comes with becoming an object, a *desired* object, is prised out of the irrationality of commodity relations.

Christina Kiaer's brilliant study *Imagine no Possessions* claims these attempts as attempted transfigurations of consumerist byt, electrifications of the high street of a fundamentally different order to fashion as we usually understand it. The objectively considered object, (*Veschch*) was the major fixation of Constructivists in their forays into industrial production: Stepanova and Popova's fabrics were mass-produced and cheap, with standardisation made a virtue – yet the designs were also jarring, bright, exciting and unlike anything being produced in the West at the time. And they were popular: by the mid-20s, 'without knowing it, all Moscow was wearing fabrics which Popova had designed'[135]. Theoretically, this was opposed to the fashioning of the body in the sense of mystique and couture's cyclical irrationalism, but not in the sense of style. Their more experimental designs, those that didn't make it into production, stressed a sexualised androgyny in the cut, coexisting with the abstractions on the surface, undermining the chauvinistic certainties of a workerist aesthetic. Kiaer's gloss on Stepanova's fashion theories notes that 'clothes would fall out of use, not because they start to look funny when the market generates novel fashions, but rather because the conditions of *byt* will have changed, necessitating new forms of clothing'[136]

Make Way for Winged Eros!

'I'm fed
to the teeth
with agitprop,
I'd like
to scribble for you
love-ballads,
they're charming,
and pay quite a lot.
But I
mastered myself
and crushed under foot
the throat
of my very own songs'
Vladimir Mayakovsky, 'At the Top of my Voice!' (1930).[137]

A sleevenote, touching in its combination of the politically and amorously earnest, on an entirely forgotten post-Dexys record from the mid-90s, asked: 'would you agree never to fall in love again if it meant the miners winning in 1985 or a Labour victory with a socialist manifesto behind it?'[138] And would you? Would I? Why is this the choice? In the year or so before his suicide, Vladimir Mayakovsky, revolutionary poet and zealous Constructivist, wrote two plays for the theatre of Vsevelod Meyerhold, both of which would be condemned by the press and regarded with suspicion by the censor. The first of these was *The Bedbug*, performed in 1929, with sets and costumes by Rodchenko and music by Shostakovich, seemingly the Soviet avant-garde in full force. However the play is full of doubt, rancour and bitter satire, caught between a shabby present and an antiseptic future. Prisypkin is a typical product of the compromised semi-capitalism of the NEP, an ex-worker done rather well who 'fought the revolution for the good life'[139] – and a heartbreaker, jilting women here and there and having a grandiose wedding to a well-fed bourgeoise ('both her breasts weigh eighty pounds each'[140]). He is interrupted in his carousing, frozen and awakened in 1979, after the triumph of the world revolution.

What happens next will be familiar to fans of Woody Allen's very similar *Sleeper*, with its orgasmatrons and comically icy rationalism. Prisypkin is reunited with one of the women who he spurned, and who attempted suicide in response – now an ageing scientist, baffled that she was ever interested in his melodrama and sentimentality. Yet these very qualities spread through the new society like the diseases carried by the bedbug that accompanies him in defrosting. 'The professors say it's an acute attack of the ancient disease they called 'love'. This was a state in which a person's sexual energy, instead of being rationally distributed over the whole of his life, was compressed into a single week and concentrated into one hectic process. This made him commit the most absurd and irresponsible acts.' He becomes a museum piece, carefully fumigated so that his absurdities don't spread. Passers-by declare 'I'd better not look. I can feel those 'love' microbes infecting the air!'[141] Prisypkin demands an art with a 'melting feeling'[142], which can't be found in the new world. Mayakovsky essentially traps himself: he can't bear the 'petrified crap of the present' and the sentiment and possessiveness of its sexuality, yet the future dreamt of by the Constructivists, biomechanicists and rationalists purges love in favour of a strictly utilitarian sexuality which is barely an improvement.

Mayakovsky had tried to unite Constructivism and an illusionless Romanticism for much of the 1920s, and in *The Bedbug* you can hear him giving up in frustration, as in his penultimate poem 'At the Top of My Voice'. This play, in its atypical ambiguity, is in part something of an argument with Sergei Tretiakov – Mayakovsky's co-editor at *New LEF* with whom he had fallen out over the role for poetry under Socialism. Tretiakov had, also for Meyerhold, attempted his own forensic analysis of love in a Communist society in the play *I Want a Child!* (1926): in which 'love is placed on an operating table.' A female Party member chooses an appropriately handsome and powerful worker to father a child, on the condition that he renege all rights over either her or the child. Although according to Kiaer's analysis of the play, the conclusions reached are ambiguous, in his introduction to a mooted screenplay of 1928 Tretiakov sounds much like those who would scrupulously avoid 'love microbes', intending that in the future it 'will be possible to return to conception the purity, all the clarity and social responsibility, that it lost choking in orgasms and gonococci.'[143] What we have here is a kind of Platonic fucking, in which a couple may 'do our duty to the Party.'[144]

However it doesn't necessarily have to be like this. An oft-trotted out Slavoj Zizek anecdote concerns some young dissident Lacanian Yugoslav types asking a Party apparatchik if he makes love to his wife like a Communist. His affirmative reply is, apparently, ridiculous: but we should ask why this should be, and why the idea of Communist sex is so risible. At the heart of the project of demystification that accompanies the left Modernist project is a demystification of Love. However, this demystification is too frequently an abandonment or a fear of love altogether, an avoidance of it – the sense that it is somehow uncomfortable. The voice in the other speaker in the Gang of Four's 'Anthrax', nervously setting out its stall, is one of the best instances of this: 'these groups think they appeal to everyone by singing about love because apparently everyone has or can love or so they would have you believe anyway but these groups go along with the belief that love is deep in everyone's personality and I don't think we're saying there's anything wrong with love just don't think that what goes on between two people should be shrouded in mystery'.[145] The defensive peevishness of this almost occludes its very sound political point: as the voice in the other speaker describes its emasculation, love becomes a source of weakness, against true revolutionary uprightness: think also of Public Enemy's declaration 'your general subject LOVE is MINIMAL - it's sex for profit'.[146]

Is there a way out of this? A demystification in which one can be in love, or a love without illusions? One Lacanian suggestion here that seems strikingly reactionary is a sort of revival of Courtly Love: a sort of endless seduction with no assumption of consummation, a sort of sex-economic counterpart to the pomo horror of teleology, to which the Reichian fetish for the cataclysmic orgasm actually seems rather preferable. The other contemporary options all seem equally grim: the aggressive alliance of the curtain-twitchingly perverse and the censoriously traditionalist that seems to characterise sexual politics in Britain, described by one wag as 'Pruritant'; a simple carrying on as before, where the old marriage contract is secularised into the mortgage; and so forth. We suffer from a sort of degeneration of the sexual-utopian imaginary: here it is no easier to imagine the end of jealousy or marriage than it is for us to imagine the end of capitalism.

From Sexpol to Sexploitation

> 'I expect the main thing that surprises you is that I sleep with men because I like them, before I've had the time to fall in love with them. But don't you see, you need to have Leisure in order to fall in love – I've read enough novels to know just how much time and energy it takes to fall in love and I just don't have the time. At the moment we've got a really enormous load of work on our hands in the district. Come to think of it, have we ever had any spare time over these last few years?'
> Alexandra Kollontai, 'Three Generations' (1923)[147]

Sexpol had a few brief cinematic incarnations: *Kuhle Wampe*, as mentioned, Leontine Sagan's glorious anti-authoritarian lesbian

Still from Makavejev's Switchboard Operator

parable *Mädchen in Uniform*, and most obscure, Abram Room's *Bed and Sofa*, scripted by Viktor Shklovsky. This 1927 film tackles the question of the old patriarchal Byt living on in the new society, via a Moscow ménage-a-trois in which Communists prove no more immune to jealousy than others, and homosociality fights off universalism. *Bed and Sofa's* critique of the half-way to paradise runs parallel to Reich's in *The Sexual Revolution*, in that all the legislation in the world can't obliterate the sexual tensions of a cramped, sweaty Kommunalka.[148] The film is an exemplary Marxist-Modernist work in its depiction of mystified things overwhelming people, with curtains, lace, film star magazines and revolutionary nick-nacks (a Stalin calendar, most memorably) all conspiring against the central character's vain hope that someone might love her like a Communist. In the end she escapes both men, for a future of single motherhood, perhaps not the conclusion a Reich or a Kollontai would have hoped for. Yet Sexpol's second entry into cinematic history would be both more strident and, curiously, more commercially successful.

There is a story of the permeation of pornography into mainstream cinema and into everyday life, and it goes much like this – a combination of American exploitation directors and French arthouse in the early 1970s, through a conjunction of fake orgasms and truck drivers on the one hand plus soft focus and cod-philosophy on the other takes what was previously only (cinematically) available in back-streets or brothels and places it in the heart of the multiplex. In this narrative the heroes are the hucksters behind *Deep Throat* or the faux-sophisticates of

Emmanuelle. These are two films from which one can trace a line to the frat film, the overlit, shaved and airbrushed horrors of most American porn and that 'another round of whispering on a bed'[149], the French sex drama, always aiming to reveal some essential truth or other. The confirmation seemingly of Michel Foucault's admonition that 'sex is boring'. Even in these histories, credit or precedence is often given to Russ Meyer for 1968's *Vixen*, one of the earliest soft-porn films to break through. It's an interesting film, not only for the usual pile-up of demented Eisensteinian montage, stupid men and huge domineering women, but also for how it inadvertently reveals what actually opened the door for the film's semi-mainstream status. One montage juxtaposes Erika Gavin contorting preposterously alongside an intense conversation between an Irish revolutionary and a black American draft dodger, one of whom is attempting to persuade the other of the merits of the Cuban road to socialism. This use of the tropes of the New Left is a possible reaction by the always canny Meyer to the huge success the previous year of *I am Curious Yellow*, a film now rather difficult to imagine.

This is the film that first shook the censors. Vilgot Sjöman's 1967 picture is a cut up of detailed, lengthy documentary discussions of the Swedish road to socialism and a semi-fictional story of the love affairs of a psychologically conflicted young woman, often interrupted by interjections from the domineering director. Where the film dissents from what would become the theoretical orthodoxy is that it politicises the simulated sex onscreen, making uncomfortable correlations between the political radicalism and sexual adventurism it depicts. Both are made ambiguous, contested. The film takes all kinds of closed off inter-war battles, principally those stemming from the Verfremdungseffekt of Brecht, the Kino-Pravda of Dziga Vertov and the sex-economy of Wilhelm Reich, and consciously or otherwise, attempts to reactivate them.[150] Whether all this was considered relevant by its US audience in 1967 is an arguable point, but for whatever reason the film caused a furore more notable than the many similarly titled bits of Swedish smut found in the any backstreet cinema: narrowly avoiding a total ban, the film is still considered pivotal in US censorship history and was its highest-grossing foreign film for 30 years. Something was happening here outside of the acceptable form of 'natural' prurience that was already making inroads to the mainstream. Rather, what made *I am Curious Yellow* so notorious was the return of the spectre of Sexpol. The decline

of bourgeois sexual mores via Sexpol's communalisation was, as we've seen, perceived by Reich at the time to be tentatively creating in the USSR 'the economic outlines of a future sex hygiene of the masses', sexually matter of fact without prurience, which was halted by Stalinism. That this returns in the tentative steps to socialism of the Swedish mixed economy in the late 60s is unsurprising. So too, in the culture of Yugoslavian 'self-management socialism'.

Still from Makavejev's WR - Mysteries of the Organism

The censorship battles faced by *I am Curious Yellow* were paralleled by Dušan Makavejev's films *The Switchboard Operator* (1967) and *WR - Mysteries of the Organism* (1970), which similarly resurrect the Reichian spectre along with the techniques of the Constructivist avant-garde, though are far sharper and less dated than Sjöman's film. The two films were sporadically banned, with the latter having the rare honour of suppression in both communist and capitalist countries (as did Reich himself) and is still only available in the UK in a bowdlerised version. The earlier of the two films is coldly striking in its combination of perversity and sobriety. Given the cumbersome but telling original title *Love*

Dossier – the Tragedy of a Switchboard Operator, it plays constantly with official discourse, be it police or medical. Open with the question, asked again after its abandonment after the 1920s; 'will man be remade?' Cut to an (actual) lecture by an ageing, diminutive sexologist, giving what will become the New Left orthodoxy of the naturalness of sexuality, to be demolished by Foucault a few years later with much glee. With a tone that suggests the discussion of the finer points of flora and fauna as much as it does human sexuality, we are told of the freedom from repression of other cultures, who even have a place for sex in their religions, of how sexuality has always been a subject for artists, not out of pleasure, mind, but out of 'an interest in man's environment' – cut to a montage of pornographic engravings and Roman phalluses (these, presumably, would be what stopped the film getting a certificate on its first release in Britain). Cut from this to the nominal story.

We are now in the heart of mid-60s consumer sexuality, listening in on two fashionably dressed young women, working in the centre of (now obsolete) communications technology that is the switchboard, facilitating technologically the old stories of amores and interrupted dialogues. The two girls walk around gossiping about their sexual history, in a city marked by traffic noise, glass and steel, noticeable only as non-'western' when the girls see a poster of Mao having his tie put on by some adoring children, then a huge banner of Lenin being unfurled over a building. While over the soundtrack a deafening Party anthem plays, we see an odd parade, the street being lined with floats of consumer goods, a giant tube of toothpaste. Cut again, this time to one of these young women being pulled naked from a well, then to a criminologist, whose manner, though somewhat more swaggering, evokes that of the sexologist – the same list of data, the same collections of curios in the service of the argument. So we already know what is going to happen to one of these women, and we are asked to make the assumption that their obvious

89

sexuality is in some way the cause of their demise.

Particularly, we begin with a mistrust of the lover she takes, Ahmed, who is a shy Bosnian Party member and former partisan now working as a ratcatcher. Our immediate suspicion, and association of sex and death, become more and more difficult to sustain in the calm serenity of the film's sex scenes, depicted with an undemonstrative slowness, the two suspended from the bombastic Party festivals going on outside. In the scene where Isabella, who we know is imminently going to be killed, seduces Ahmed, she uses a 'wonderful old Soviet film' being shown on television as bait of some sort. Cut to the film, which is in fact Dziga Vertov's behemoth of revolution's *Enthusiasm*, and specifically its montage of the destruction of churches. While we know the two are fucking in the background, the film plays and we see the steeples of churches, pointing at phallic angles via the vertiginous camera angles, shaking until being torn down to huge cheers, punctuating until the final hoisting of a red flag over the church – and the lovers, sated.

Makavejev uses Vertov's own methods of defamilarisation and disjointed montage, his marshalling of fact into obviously formed works, and suggests the elements of society Vertov himself didn't quite mention. Another artefact from the Soviet avant-garde might be a correlative, the eroticised montage of Alexander Dovzhenko's *Earth*, in the curious section where a grief-ridden, seemingly sexually explosive naked woman tearing at the contents of a room symbolises the class struggle. Except that here our couple's sexual ease is what is remarkable, such as in the rather touching scenes of quotidian life that make up much of the film – cooking, showering together, and memorably pottering around a courtyard to the sound of Ernst Busch, star of *Kuhle Wampe*, stridently singing a Mayakovsky poem set to music. Hanns Eisler's strident and swinging music and the declarations that the movement is going 'forwards in time!' sit disjunctively but appropriately with the carnal idyll set up here.

This matter-of-fact carnality is interrupted again and again, here by the details of Isabella's autopsy, there by some found footage of prettily innocent 1900s films where titillation is covered by mythological poses. Through to the eventual denouement, the death of Isabella (which is not quite what we expect) the implication is constantly that here, on these mundane everyday levels, is where the struggle is most important, as opposed to the demonstrative official showcases of solidarity we occasionally glimpse. That this ends so unhappily is the end result of Makavejev's schematicism: here is the missing element, without which socialism is meaningless. This critique at a vastly more explicit level and a conception of montage that even Eisenstein would have found a little overenthusiastic is what marks the subsequent *WR - Mysteries of the Organism*.

I Still Dream of Orgonon

"You know, it seemed to me just now that I was holding your whole youthful world in my arms. Its despotism, its egoism, its desperate hunger for happiness – I felt all that in your caresses. Your love is like murder. But – I love you, Lenni."
The Martian Netti to Leonid in Bogdanov's *Red Star* (1908)[151]

WR is so dense with allusions, groaning under the weight of its own intertextuality, that it's almost impossible to truly encompass, particularly as the critique is here widened to the totality of late 60s society, in particular in the USA and (naturally) Yugoslavia. But a divide could be made, roughly Reich biopic/contemporary USA/Yugoslav fiction. We open with footage of a 'Filme der Sexpol', a pink kaleidoscope showing the sylvan fucking of a Weimar couple over quotes from Reich himself and a song trilling 'Communist Party, to me you are as fragrant flowers', then onto a reasonably straight documentary on our hero. This evokes Chris Marker in its density of montage and refusal to impose an interpretation of its footage. Small town shopkeepers discuss Reich's haircut. An Orgone accumulator is demonstrated. Orgone therapy is documented, its calmness and sudden ferocity disturbs. We hear the story of Reich's conversion from Communism to his own anti-Stalinist (which to him was 'Red Fascism') theory of 'work democracy', to the Orgone experiments and his death partly at the hands of the American state (and after he'd voted for Eisenhower!). In the Orgonon commune Reich's widow confronts Makavejev, accuses him of being a Stalinist. He asks her if she'd prefer the American model of freedom. 'No! The American dream is dead!' We see a man dressed as an urban guerrilla running round New York, past utterly unfazed citizens.

The film's centre then emerges, the figure of the heroic Reichian prophet Milena, who we first see reading a party paper, dumping her unreconstructed proletarian lover ('remnant of our glorious past!'), and benignly noting her flatmate fucking a young conscript crying 'forward, people's army!' We see the consumer communist society of *The Switchboard Operator* tottering, as said ex-lover builds barricades against the 'red bourgeoisie', fights police, and she turns a walk round her apartment block into a Reichian sermon against Stalinist sexual oppression. Dressed in a uniform, she calls at a growing crowd 'free love is where the October revolution failed…politics attracts those whose orgasm is incomplete!' The tenants link arms and sing ribald versions of party anthems and she is carried aloft as Communist heroine. Cut to the frenzy of Chinese red guards. Cut to the sound of 'Lili Marleen' and a piece of tinted film footage. This is *The Vow*, from the period of Soviet filmmaking where Stalin was the obligatory hero (the difference between Stalin and Tarzan is that people don't consider films about the latter to be factual, said Andre Bazin). 'Stalin' looks resolute. Cut to a horrifying, lingering shot of electroshock therapy. Cut again to (another) sexologist. 'I don't have a body, I *am* a body', he says after this depiction of terrible physical extremity.

Then we have a romance. Milena meets a people's artist. His name is Vladimir Ilyich, and he's a Russian dancer. Though her friends don't approve of his 'revolutionary art in the costumes of Tsarism' she is smitten. So we see her and friends try and convert him to their self-management sexpol. Milena tries everything to shock Vladimir Ilyich, she compares Reich and that other Soviet unperson Leon Trotsky: W.R is 'World Revolution' as well as 'Wilhelm Reich'. Her naked flatmate waves her legs in the air. He calmly says 'this sounds like the theory of Alexandra Kollontai that revolution does away with marriage', implying the USSR has transcended such frippery. 'You want permanent revolution and permanent orgasm.' Her ex-lover crashes through the wall and locks Vladimir Ilyich in a cupboard, which we soon discover is in fact an Orgone Accumulator. Milena seems blithely unconcerned at this violating of the walls of her apartment by 'highly skilled worker Radmilovic': as we've seen in her apartment block agitprop, private space is, for her, always convertible into public space, whose inhabitants can be marshalled into those lusty versions of Party chants.

Cut again. We're back in New York, and a radio DJ is advocating eliminating the Black Panthers via ethnic cleansing, as 'they breed faster than us'. Makavejev's picture of the US is one of the most fascinating of outsiders' perspectives, gleefully taking down what others wouldn't notice – the inanity and ideology of advertising, especially the one for 'beautiful blinkers', montaged over the figure of the transsexual and Warhol superstar Jackie Curtis eating an ice cream. Makavejev notes the promises of utopia of figures like Curtis, nonchalantly glamorous, trashing the limits of gender and impossible anywhere else, depicted holding his/her fist aloft in front of the Stars & Stripes, but alongside the idiocies and barbarism of the Vietnam war and the pointless abundances of US capitalism. A song playing over the footage implores 'kill, kill, kill for peace'. Interestingly, the respect he has for Curtis isn't mirrored in his treatment of the mock-sexpol of parts of the New Left. We see rather too much of Jim Buckley, the editor of *Screw*, a porn mag which he is at pains to impress upon us as quintessentially American, all about *freedom*. Though the intersection of porn and politics is what makes these films so interesting, the more dubious end of post-68 sexpol is not

overlooked here: the notion that somehow onanism is a part of the struggle. We see (or rather in the current English version we *don't* see) Buckley having his cock plaster-casted to a voice drawling 'I'll kill myself over your dead body, if you fuck anybody but me'; then cut again to *The Vow* and the sombre yet heroic and

Still from Makavejev's WR - Mysteries of the Organism

upright 'Stalin'. Power cutting across the alleged dividing line of the Iron Curtain.

The corpus of Bolshevism has both impulses within it. Milena and Vladimir Ilyich argue with each other in quotes from Lenin; she throws at him the famous lines from *The State & Revolution* that 'when freedom exists there will be no state', he fires back his claim that listening to the Appassionata makes one want to 'pat on the head' one's enemies rather than destroying them. Another scene from *The Vow* makes plain the evils linking the two societies, as 'Stalin', to glutinous music resembling that of 1940s Hollywood, facing an adoring crowd in Red Square, is handed a note by a little old lady asking him to fulfil Lenin's work – then another harsh edit to Milena crying at V.I 'you love all mankind, but you're incapable of loving an individual'. Soon, another of Makavejev's autopsies, a severed head calmly denouncing Soviet 'red fascism', but declaring 'even now I am not ashamed of my Communist past'.

Cinema's experiments in Sexpol are now as distant as the Reichian Communism that runs through all these films, except in the more detailed histories of banned movies. Because of this, we've lost their fundamental point that the sexual

Still from Makavejev's WR - Mysteries of the Organism

'honesty' we all now take for granted is part of a wider political project and is completely meaningless without it. The films do titillate, and are very much designed to do so – no invocations of the categories 'art' or 'erotica' here – although one would find the digressions on political morality and psychoanalytic theory somewhat distracting if looking for straightforward skinflicks, they are all part of the same totality, part of an easily dismissed movement that has within it the hints of what is missing from our current body politic.

Above all, *WR* is a supremely total presentation of the internal debate within Marxism and the Marxist avant-garde itself, against its repressive proponents and for its original promises. Raymond Durgnat's slim book on *WR* notes that the film is a recapitulation of a meeting that never took place between Reich and the Soviet avant-garde's biomechanical wing. 'In 1934 Eisenstein asked Reich for his *Orgasm* book, and whether or not one links Eisenstein's interest in 'ecstasy' with Milena's just before she dies, Eisenstein's 'biomechanics', his sensitivity to the physical body, and his theories of 'non-indifferent nature' parallel Reich.'[152] But as he points out, in another parallel, 'even (Soviet Marxism's) libertarian phase (free love, instant divorce) was geared to theories of sex as stimulus-response.'[153] Is the liberated sexuality proposed by Tretiakov's *I Want a Child*, by Reich's Sexpol or by Makavejev's Milena not rather akin to Greta Garbo's *Ninotchka*? Billy Wilder's script has this Soviet 'new woman' being *sachlich* about sex as a physical relaxant and pleasure but suspicious of love – and ready to crumble at ballgowns, Tsarist jewellery and all the trappings of bourgeois seduction. Can we love without myth? Alexandra Kollontai, when she declared that socialism will 'make way for winged eros'[154] in a way that a society based on property never could, would certainly have said so. Sexpol's spectre is still haunting the bedrooms and the psyches of late capitalism, and lingers perhaps for all those who have what Andreas Baader called 'revolutionary orgasm problems': the inability, or unwillingness, to find the required 'fulfilment' in a prurient puritanism.

4: Alienation Affects

Brechtian Productivism in an age of Mechanical Stagnation

Art forms also die. And the rotting corpse that is the theatre has, for the last 20 years or more, been involved in a comprehensive occlusion, distortion and demolition of the work of one of the 20th century playwrights who attempted to keep it alive. But in that attempt, regardless of whether the theatre lives or dies, is a theory of the technological apparatus, and of production, that still speaks of demands that the proliferating media of today seem incapable of fulfilling. The theatre itself disdains these theories and these techniques. Why?

Godot Vs Galileo

> *'Mr Keuner ran into Mr Muddle, a great fighter against newspapers. 'I am a great opponent of newspapers. I don't want any newspapers', said Mr Muddle. Mr Keuner said 'I am a greater opponent of newspapers. I want better newspapers.'*
>
> *If newspapers are a means to disorder, then they are also a means to achieving order. It is precisely people like Mr Muddle who through their dissatisfaction demonstrate the value of newspapers. Mr Muddle thinks he is concerned with the worthlessness of today's newspapers. In fact he is concerned with their worth tomorrow.*
>
> *Mr Muddle thought highly of man and did not believe that newspapers could be made better, whereas Mr Keuner did not think very highly of man but did think that newspapers could be made better. 'Everything can be made better', said Mr Keuner, 'except man.'*
> Brecht, *Stories of Herr Keuner*[155]

A juxtaposition might help elucidate this little conundrum. 2006 was the 100th anniversary of the birth of Samuel Beckett, as well as the 50th anniversary of the death of Bertolt Brecht. The difference between the reception of these two anniversaries in Britain was striking. While Beckett was beset with tributes, seasons, retrospectives, those chiselled features looking out from arts centres all over, Brecht was very grudgingly acknowledged. A few productions have appeared, and each one of them has had the same mission statement: to take the Brechtian out of Brecht, to extract from it all that pernicious theorising and return it to the cathartic, realist stage. From the National Theatre's *Life of Galileo*, which explicitly tried to make a regular middlebrow tale of compromised liberalism out of the alienation effects, to a Young Vic 'Big Brecht Fest' which went so far as to expunge works that post-dated the development of Brechtian 'theory' in 1926-7, there has been an unrelenting attack on Brecht's technique – which usually accompanies rhetoric about what a *Great Artist* he was despite all this.

Brecht knew that Beckett was essentially his dramatic inverse, and was planning a 'response' play to *Waiting for Godot* at the time of his death in 1956. The Brechtian and the Beckettian are both paths that the post-war theatre could have taken, and it seems he at least was aware of this. Of course, since the 70s neither direction has been followed.[156] Nonetheless, while Adorno in his 1962 attack on Brecht and Sartre's 'Commitment' argued that while these aspiring agitators could be easily reified and turned into cliché, Beckett or Kafka, 'autonomous' artists, could resist such treatment.[157] The reverse has actually proved to be the case. What is perceived as Beckett's depiction of a grim, sardonic struggle against an immutable human condition has an obvious appeal for a stagnant, fatalist and depoliticised terminal capital (alternatively, go to post-Stalinist Prague to find Kafka's name emblazoned on anything with a price tag) while Brecht's insistence on the critical stance is utterly anathema to its tamed culture. And this is usually stated in terms of pleasure, or enjoyment: the Brechtian technique is allegedly something that ensures aridity, its laying bare of the device merely leading to a dry formalism. It's *no fun*.

Really, Brecht has so little going for him here it's almost comic: Marxist, German, Hegelian, his innovations summed up as either the rather grand sounding 'Epic Theatre' or theorised in imposingly Teutonic terms as the *'Verfremdungseffekt'* which is seemingly designed to be oppressive: whether you translate it as 'alienation' or 'distanciation' or 'estrangement', it isn't a phrase that promises a whole load of fun. But what is so frustrating about this is that it simply doesn't square with any of what either Beckett or Brecht *actually wrote*. Beckett's *Late Review* devotees seem to have an idea of him as some sort of amalgam of Zeno the Stoic and Father Ted, yet one can't imagine Tom Paulin or Bonnie Greer relishing being assaulted by the panic attack of *Not I* or wading through the thick, impenetrable tangle of repetition and horror of *How it Is*. Beckett is not fun. For all his virtues, he is a supremely difficult writer, almost all of his mature works extremely forbidding: one might extract a quote or two from *Worstward Ho*, but few try reading the bastard thing. To be crass, people think they would like Beckett but wouldn't, and think they wouldn't like Brecht – but they would.

Brecht's works, curiously enough, are absolutely full of singing, dancing, rhythm, laugh-out-loud jokes, wickedly biting irony, and perhaps most importantly, a refusal to ever be *boring*. The obvious pleasures of the Kurt Weill assisted musicals of 1927-33 (*Seven Deadly Sins, Threepenny Opera, Happy End, Mahogonny*) almost seem to go without saying, their songs' persistent presence in pop culture ever since being proof enough of that: yet this was the exact period of the development of the Marxist-Modernist Brechtian apparatus of interruption and interjection, the placards and projections that everyone seems to so object to. Even the *lehrstücke* ('learning plays'), his most stripped down and didactically severe pieces – most notoriously the 'wild roar' (Adorno) of *The Measures Taken* – have an extremism, a starkness and violence, that prevent them from ever becoming mere academic experiments. So, we will have to ask, what is it in the Brechtian conceptual apparatus that makes people want to separate it from the work? Why is this device that must be laid bare so forbidding to the arbiters of taste? And more to the point, what are these theories, how do they work, and what do they have to do with film and the media rather than the stage?

Who's Afraid of the Verfremdungseffekt?

> *'They are the enemies of production. Production makes them uncomfortable. You never know where you are with production. Production is the unforeseeable'*[158]
> Brecht, on Socialist Realism

Like any theory worth investigating, the Brechtian Methodologies morphed and changed to respond to new conditions, but perhaps most interesting for our purposes here is the period from the mid 20s to mid 30s, when the development of Brecht's technique was explicitly linked with *Technik* (i.e., the German term for Technology). Walter Benjamin defined the alienation effect, the form of the Epic Theatre, as first and foremost an engagement with the new reified art forms of the 20th century, and specifically film and radio. In 'Theatre and Radio' a piece for the *Blatter des Hessischen Landstheaters* in 1932, Benjamin writes of the mass form of radio, its ability to reach a greater audience than even the most populist theatre, giving it potentialities which the stage can't approach.

> 'Not only a more advanced technical stage, but also one in which technology is more evident. Unlike the theatre, it does not have a classical age behind it. The masses it grips are much

larger; above all, the material elements on which its apparatus is based are closely intertwined with the interests of its audience. Confronted with this, what can the theatre offer? The use of live people – and apart from this, nothing.'[159]

There are two possible responses to this. One is that of Great Artists, where this simply doesn't matter because of the eternal nature of the human condition. The other response is to acknowledge that the theatre can't compete with cinema and radio, but can however debate with them. And it does this, crucially, via Montage. The alienation effect is

'Nothing but a retranslation of the methods of montage – so crucial in radio and film – from a technological process to a human one. It is enough to point out that the principle of the Epic Theatre, like that of montage, is based on interruption'

and via that interruption, the listener has to 'take up an attitude towards the events on stage': the laying bare of the device induces a stance. An early play of Brecht's featured the banner 'DON'T STARE SO ROMANTICALLY': instead the audience has to assume a critical engagement.

Benjamin develops this two years later in 'The Author as Producer'[160], where the properties of this montage are further discussed: 'the superimposed element disrupts the context in which it is inserted'. So here we have a picture of the Epic Theatre where the Verfremdungseffekt is essentially an adaptation to new technological realities, and a harnessing of them specifically for the theatre (but not exclusively so) in order to disrupt its attempts to claim that the world goes on as before. The theory can in fact be adapted for use in Film and in Radio: as Brecht was doing at the time, producing with collectives of collaborators, composers and designers radio productions such as *The Flight of the Lindberghs*. Here the most impressive new technological achievement of the time, the transatlantic flight, is made a collaboration between collective producers building the plane, each one of whom is 'Lindbergh'; or in stage plays, an apparatus is introduced making prominent use of radio, newspaper headlines or projections of photographs and statistics.

Brecht's theory and practice here was closely linked to two Soviet theoretical innovations, produced by the circle around the journal *LEF*. This was the far Left of Constructivism, usually calling themselves 'Productivists' (in the sense of productive, producing, and the product). First of all the notion of 'making strange', developed by the Formalist literary theorists such as Viktor Shklovsky and Osip Brik, who were also prolific Screenplay writers for directors like Pudovkin and Room; and the development by Sergei Tretiakov and others of the notion of the Operative writer who is at once a sociologist, photographer, economist, filmmaker, producer, master of the new apparatus; and the linked experiments like the 'Two-Way Newspaper'. The producers becoming artists and the artists becoming producers.[161] Brecht wrote in 1927 that the new technological forms had just this radical potential for mass access and communication. In 'The Radio as a Communications Apparatus'[162] he writes:

'Among the obligations of the state's highest official is the job of informing the nation regularly by means of the radio about his activities and their justification. The task of the radio does not end, however, with the transmission of these reports.

Beyond this, it must organise the collection of reports, i.e. it must transform the reports of those who govern into responses to the questions of those governed. Radio must make exchange possible.

Should you consider this utopian, then I ask you to reflect on the reasons why it is utopian.'

Capitalism has to prevent this apparatus from falling into the hands of all, a radical democratisation of cultural production disrupting the divide between art and life upon which the supremacy of its culture industry depends. The Epic Theatre can't redistribute the apparatus by itself – but what it can do is present it in an objective manner, show its workings and effects as what they are, to resist the temptation of using it to represent reality or history rather than participate in it. He writes in 'Suggestions for the Director of Radio Broadcasting' that because the radio's apparatus is portable, mass-produced, by its nature not exclusive, to attempt representation with it is inherently absurd. In the case of cinema, 'I have seen with distress how the Egyptian pyramids and the Indian Rajahs' palaces move to Neubabelsburg (the studios in Potsdam that were the centre of the 1920s German film industry) in order to be filmed by an apparatus that a man can slip comfortably into his backpack.'[163]

The great mistake here is to see in this an inherent hostility to mass produced culture, and to the productions of that film industry. On the contrary, while the European cinema strained for Art, the American gangster film or slapstick comedy was already devising an appropriate form for the new functional media. Take for instance the 1936 fragment 'V-Effects of Chaplin', a little comment on the employment of alienation effects in *The Gold Rush* (1925):

Eating the boot (with proper table manners, removing the nail like a chicken bone, the index finger pointing outward).
The film's mechanical aids:
Chaplin appears to his starving friend as a chicken.
Chaplin destroying his rival and at the same time courting him.'[164]

So the Verfremdungseffekt is here expressed by gesture, movement, the anti-naturalism producible by the human body

103

itself (the Brechtian gestus, what Benjamin described as the actor's critical stance towards his character) as well as by the techno-logical apparatus. The Hollywood film, at its least middlebrow edges, is capable of being just as jarring as the Epic Theatre. In the scenes from *The Gold Rush* referenced above, a situation of poverty and abjection is made strange, while at the same time made universal. The absurdity of the situation is conveyed by the anti-naturalist gesture, and by the morphing of man into chicken achievable only via the device.

According to Hanns Eisler, Brecht disdained music in favour of the invention 'Misuc': a response to a Beethoven that 'always reminds me of paintings of battles', and 'music ceremoniously produced in concert halls', replacing it with a din that is 'extremely close to the people'.[165] And as any contemporary production of Brecht will tend to renege on all of this, the best place to encounter it today is on record, in the interpretations of Brecht's songs by anyone from Lotte Lenya to Nina Simone, the Young Gods to Ernst Busch. This is fitting, as pop had its own Brechtian moment in the late 70s and early 80s, much as Cinema did in the late 60s and early 70s[166]. Some of the most straight-forward statements of the Brechtian method are on the subject of music, whether in the 'mass songs' that he wrote for the Popular Front of the 30s with Eisler, or in his writings on film music. In 1942, while working on Fritz Lang's *Hangmen Also Die*, Brecht wrote a short programmatic piece, 'On Film Music', as a contri-bution to Adorno and Eisler's study *Composing for the Films*.[167] This contains one of the most succinct statements of technique and technik. Under the heading 'Function of Innovations' Brecht writes of a technique 'directed mainly against the narcotic function of art', and one which of necessity has to be based on 'Excitement – without which theatre today can hardly be imagined'. The use of music in this was totally paramount, for the same reason that the Musical, at its most extreme (Dennis Potter, Lars von Trier) is the culture industry's most truly Brechtian form.

'Music had the task of protecting the audience from a state of 'trance'. It did not serve the enhancement of existing or antic-ipated effects but rather interrupted or manipulated them. So if there were songs in a play, it was not as if the story 'dissolved into song'. The people in the play did not break into song. On the contrary, they openly interrupted the story. They assumed a pose for singing and presented the song in a way that did not fully correspond to the situation.'

Then the audience would be taught not to trust what they see: they can 'discover the emptiness and conventionalism of certain events which the actors had played with unshakeable seriousness.'

A Threepenny Film and a Threepenny Lawsuit

'The Russian writer Osip Brik noted very cleverly that Brecht's works are always court cases, in which Brecht proves himself to have litigation-mania'
Sergei Tretiakov, 'Bert Brecht' (1934)[168]

So what happened when the Brechtian – well, when Brecht himself – was unleashed on cinema? Although in his quasi-expressionist youth Brecht had worked on unproduced screen-plays and even directed a short film, the first opportunity for his mature theory to be tested was in an adaptation of his 1928 musical *The Threepenny Opera*. This was a cobbled together melange made up of a title of Lion Feuchtwanger's, a translation and rewriting by Elisabeth Hauptmann of John Gay's *Beggar's Opera*, plus adaptations by Brecht of that play's original songs, poems by Francois Villon and Rudyard Kipling(!), and even some 'original' work, all honed via Kurt Weill's self-deconstructing music into a viciously witty depiction of amoral capitalism. Famous variety tale of murder, rape and general gangstaism

Romance is over – serious life begins

Still from G.W Pabst's The Threepenny Opera

'Mack the Knife' (or 'Moritat von Mackie Messer') hails from here, and was included specifically as a measure against an actor who was making his villain rather too worthy of identification: better to make him 'violate an old woman in her slumbers' for cash rather than let him become a straightforward hero. This chaotic, disjunctive and discordant mess of syncopated cynicism and mercenary amorousness (see 'The Ballad of Sexual Dependency') was one of the greatest popular successes of the Weimar Republic. A vindication, if ever there were, that works created in the new manner could connect just as well, if not better, with a mass audience.

This already deeply hybrid work then gets very complicated indeed. Though the work was contemporaneous with Brecht's turn towards Marxism and development of Epic Theatre, by the time the film was put into development in 1930 Brecht and his collaborators had shifted artistically and politically to the extreme left, and this was going to be for them a way of testing the new apparatus' potentialities for both political efficacy and formal rupture. A screenplay was written, entitled *The Bruise: a Threepenny Film*, which quite explicitly called for the montage experiments of Eisenstein, Pudovkin or Vertov as well as a Gestural, anti-naturalist acting style indebted to Chaplin or Keaton. That is, as opposed to the leisurely pace, fluid camera and subtle, insinuating acting styles advocated by the German Expressionist art film: one of whose number, G.W Pabst, fresh from the Weimar-Goth classic *Pandora's Box*, was slated to direct. Needless to say, Brecht's treatment was rejected, and a new screenplay was written partly by Bela Balasz, a prominent theorist of film at the time. Balasz advocated that film learn from Art, that film become Art. He was invited to show and discuss some French art films (Rene Clair, Abel Gance, Jean Renoir) in Moscow in the late 20s, eliciting a reponse from Eisenstein: 'Bela Forgets the Scissors'. These works, for all their alleged innovation, really returned film to the canvas, and to the artistic spectacle, precisely because they ignored the principle of interruption and of montage. For Eisenstein, as for Brecht, they were no 'use'.

Before going on to look at the film itself, we should have a look at the case Brecht assembles in his *Threepenny Lawsuit*.[169] This tract, assembled after Brecht had already lost his case against the film's producers, has very little to do with Pabst's film: whether or not Brecht had ever actually watched it is a moot point. In fact, it is probably the most sweeping, manifesto-like statement of the Epic Theatre in its Productivist moment. Its first target is those who, over the lawsuit, claimed that Brecht and Weill should have expected the treatment they got: film is a commodity, is not art, and as such any attempt to try and make it so (which Brecht, as a noted playwright working in the cinema, was presumed to have been doing) was doomed to failure. These people want to 'from the outset deprive us of the apparatuses which we need in order to produce, because more and more this kind of producing will supersede the present one.'

Still from G.W Pabst's The Threepenny Opera

An alternative to either this sulky aestheticism or a total surrender to the demands of capital can only be enabled by an expansion of the apparatus: in a short passage pregnant with potential Brecht imagines that the *Lehrstücke*'s participants, usually active Communists, acting anywhere other than a conventional stage, would all have to have their own personal cinema apparatus. The freedom outside the new technology is meaningless. 'To say to the intellectual worker that he is free to renounce the new work tools is to assign to him a freedom outside the production process', and hence to render him utterly neutered, no threat to things as they are.

Then there is the Third Way: film as art. This is based on a form that 'establishes itself against the apparatuses with a vengeance', the filmed theatre that Eisenstein feared the development of sound could create. 'He violates the apparatuses with his 'art'. This is linked in with the belief that if something is 'faithfully depicted', then it is in some way able to be critical, that representation can be critique. In an allusion to the lovingly shot machinery of the photographer Renger-Patzsch, he writes that a photograph of a factory 'reveals almost nothing about these institutions'. A more bastard form is needed. Here, the forms produced by the culture industry's disruptive wing are again a way of employing the apparatus, and against the claims of the art film he writes 'the masses' bad taste is rooted more deeply in reality than the intellectuals' good taste.' Cinema constantly exhibits a potentiality that, for all its employment as a mere money-making machine, can be turned on its head. Its essentially collective production is an exemplar of that: 'it is the essence of capitalism and not something generally valid that 'unique' and 'special' artefacts can only be produced by individuals and collectives only bring forth standardised mass commodities.' What if the collective and mass form could create something 'unique'?

In one of the very few allusions to the actual film that resulted from this debacle, it is claimed that Pabst, as an artist seems to have 'the right to stupidity, which is usually extended to poets, painters, musicians etc, and is in fact more of an obligation'. 76 years later, a look at Pabst's film reveals it as a more complex and murky work than Brecht would credit (if indeed he ever saw it), although it is a perfect example of what happens to these works when the theory is stripped out. According to Tretiakov, Pabst told Brecht that he wanted to make 'a beautiful fairytale' out of *The Threepenny Opera*, and this is exactly what he did. On just one of those huge mimetic sets in Potsdam that so amused Brecht, this time of a Dickensian London rather than the Pyramids, is spread out a haunted landscape of passageways and posters, smog and alleys, rats and dirt, brothels and palaces: more or less an estrangement of Weimar Berlin itself, although crucially the illusionistic nature of this is never alluded to, and the device stays resolutely unbared. The film featured many members of Brecht's collective, and the divergence of their acting styles with Pabst's (sur)realist mise-en-scene is peculiarly fascinating. A terrific Carola Neher as Polly Peachum is all gesture, whether dismissing her band of gangsters or acquiring a proto-Thatcher pomp as she becomes a bank magnate: sweeps of the hand, cocks of the head are what mark out her performance, for all Pabst's focus on her pulchritude via the frequent close-ups. Ernst Busch's street singer is wonderfully sardonic, and Lotte Lenya's moment where on her own in the brothel she sings 'Pirate Jenny', her still utterly chilling (or thrilling, depending on where you stand) fantasy of class war and gory revenge, remains shiveringly powerful. Pabst creates a seductively eerie filmworld, and one which does in its way exploit the new apparatus (all those lingering tracking shots, already becoming an arthouse motif). There's only really one major problem with it. It's *slow*.

There are several reasons for the inertia and longeurs of the film, and many of these are precise consequences of its occlusion of the Brechtian. Anything that contradicted the tangibility of the mimetic city that Pabst had built was anathema. It's a mistake to see this as it's usually posited, as a merely political question: Brecht's expansion of the 1928 play into a general indictment of capitalism is actually *retained* by Pabst, who was at this point a committed socialist. But what he couldn't countenance was the way in which *The Bruise* or the original play was so doggedly unreal: he cut over half of Weill's songs (so the composer actually won his part of the lawsuit) as people don't just start singing, do they? So somehow they have to be inserted into a realist narrative, in the process becoming static: rather than interrupting the narrative, a character will stand stock still and sing a song to occasion. The avoidance of montage, meanwhile, means that the film can start to stagnate, to ossify, and to induce the trance that the theorists of Making Strange most feared: the viewer is drugged by the slow, passive, foggy drag of Fritz Arno Wagner's camera through the fantasy London, and rather than being made to think or to engage, and rather than being excited, the spectator is induced to dream. Perhaps the disjunction between the dreamy and the cynical creates its own kind of alienation, yet when the film's final reconciliation of the gangster, the capitalist and the state occurs, the effect isn't agitational – it's fatalistic. Without the theory, a political effect is neutered.

A Short Course in Realism from the Perspective of the Police

'As artists you must forgive me the expression we learn too little about him, but the consequences are of a political nature and force me to object to the film's release. Your film proposes that suicide is typical, that it is not simply this or that (pathologically disposed) individual but rather the fate of an entire social class...no, gentlemen, you have not behaved as artists, not here. You were not interested in showing the shocking fate of an individual, which no one would prevent you from doing....Good God, the actor does it as if he were showing how to peel cucumbers'[170]

Alleged words of the Censor of *Kuhle Wampe*

The first 15 minutes of the film that the Brecht collective made a year later in response, *Kuhle Wampe*, are like being in a different century, seem to be using an entirely different apparatus to Pabst's film. First we have a stark intertitle, a montage of newspaper headlines, then we are thrown into a montage of factories and tenements, which, as Adorno and Eisler would later elucidate, had to be accompanied by a music that would not induce a picturesque aestheticism, a Hovis advert depiction of the proletarian picturesque. Instead the music is sharp, scything, desperate. Then intercut with this dilapidated city are hordes of the unemployed on bicycles, shots of their wheels, their faces as they search all over Berlin for work. Then one of the unemployed arrives home. The desperation slows, and is replaced by an unbearable inertia. A family argument, a procession of 'get on yer bike' clichés. Then our unemployed protagonist – the nearest thing we have had so far to a point of identification – takes off his watch and throws himself out of the window.

Still from Slatan Dudow's Kuhle Wampe

The way that politics and aesthetics intersected here is interesting. To the Censor who banned the film, this sudden suicide was proof of a Communist mendacity and avant-garde disdain for the human. The man was not depicted as a full human being. He was a type, a representative of a class. The Censor, according to Brecht's account quoted above, was deeply affronted by this dereliction of artistic duty. This, of course, was seen as a total vindication of the political usefulness of their techniques. Brecht wryly notes 'we had the unpleasant sensation of being caught red handed'.

There is little else like *Kuhle Wampe*, in cinema or elsewhere. In just over an hour, we have here first an experiment in avant-garde montage and music. The alienation effects extend to cut-ups of decidedly experimental 'Misuc' over advertising and strangely threatening children (as a character contemplates an unwanted pregnancy), then second we have a kitchen sink drama. One of the collective here, Ernst Ottwald, was one of the 'proletarian novelists' of the late 20s, who included factography and sociological analysis in their narratives, much to the chagrin of Socialist Realists. The depiction of working class life is extremely rare in being critical without patronising. The older members of the family at the centre of the play are crippled by ingrained phrases and automatic responses to events that stop them from ever having to truly think about their situation. Their tiny flat, and subsequently their tent in the film's titular camp, is full of phantasmagoric objects, nick-nacks and shoddily Imperial remnants: leftovers of the bourgeoisie. This isn't presented in the manner of a sniffy disdain for their bad taste, but its absurdity is calmly laid out. Their inability to make the connections between their fate and what goes on outside is encapsulated beautifully in the scene where the father laboriously reads from the newspaper a lurid article on the erotic adventures of Mata Hari, while the mother writes out a shopping list, her terror at her inability to make ends meet depicted through a montage of price tags and consumer goods.

Third, we have here a propaganda film on two fronts. Through the depiction of a Communist festival there is a demonstration of working class power; and through the escape of the film's central character (played by Hertha Thiele) from a stifling, lumpen environment, there is a depiction of the radicalisation of *alltagsleben*. A politicised everyday life necessitates a new sexual politics, and with the help of her more committed friends, she is able to escape the future of drudgery that is usually reserved for women of her class. Then, fourth, we have an argument in a U-

Bahn train. This is a precedent to one of the better elements in the Socialist Realist cinema of today, an analogue to the remarkable scene in Ken Loach's *Land and Freedom* where a room full of people discuss the nationalisation of agriculture without it becoming tedious. A political argument with wit, cut and thrust, inducing the audience to think about the issues critically rather than accept the director's perspective. So in a public spat over coffee being burnt in South America, there are absurdist non-sequiteurs, political agitation, and a variety of perspectives critically evaluated. The interruption ceases in this scene, but in order to induce thought rather, as with Pabst, than to occlude it.

The most remarkable thing about *Kuhle Wampe* though is the sheer *joy* of the film. In a similar (only so much less violent) manner to Eisenstein's theory of the Montage of Attractions, where agitational cinema is achieved via a panoply of exciting effects, the film's full-to-bursting turnover of styles and effects, wit and pathos, kitchen sink realism and formal experimentation keep it for the most part in a state of continuous agitation and libidinal charge. The scenes of the Communist sports festival are perhaps key here. Eisler's music shifts from its peculiar special effects and grimly sweeping themes to stirring songs, stridently belted out by the poignant baritone of Ernst Busch (who also plays the male lead, an apolitical mechanic), which speak of movement, participation, of learning in preparation for taking power. The difference between the mass festival here and that filmed by Riefenstahl later in the decade is enormous. Everyone is jostling, talking to each other, discussing, thinking and acting at once. These are the inheritors of history, and the future, going 'forwards, not forgetting' as the refrain goes.

Kuhle Wampe's hybridity was paralleled elsewhere by Eisler, in his work with the KPD's cultural organisations. There's an uncanniness in reading Eisler's early-30s ideas, given how they return in a mutated form later in the century in mass media, especially in pop and its experimental fringes: from the

No, it wasn't, it was that one

Still from Slatan Dudow's Kuhle Wampe

prophecy of 'Industrial' that is 'Blast Furnace Music' to an extraordinary programme for a sort of working class montage gesamtkunstwerk. In 'Music for Workers' Orchestras' (1932-3), we find the recommendation that, after choosing songs, the workers' choir should 'confer with the revolutionary writers, agitprop groups, workers photography circles and the Marxist workers' school, explaining the purpose of the performance. The Marxist workers' school should be asked to provide a speaker; and a small working team consisting of representatives from the orchestra, the choir, the writers, the agitprop group and the photography circle should work out a program. This should consist of a loose sequence of scenes, fighting songs, choral and orchestral pieces, 16mm films and projected documentary photos. This production should be mounted partly from already existing material (and therefore it is called montage in Germany).'

This is a kind of Red precursor to the overwhelming total media spectacles of the 1960s, a Communist Exploding Plastic Inevitable: only here the 'everyone is an artist' ethos is insurrectionary rather than blank and wan. The purpose is not to dazzle but to demystify cultural production. Eisler goes on: 'in such a way the workers' orchestras can offer first-class performances, since our new revolutionary style of music enables novel and original compositions to be so contrived that they can also be well executed by untrained amateurs.'[171] This isn't just a formal preference for disjunctions. If it can be truly *used*, all manner of material can be bent and reshaped into an instrument for struggle – take what is useful and throw away what isn't. With reference to jazz, for instance, Eisler suggests taking the rhythm but certainly not the melody.[172] Mass culture is a mine of possibilities, but never something to uncritically embrace.

The Half That's Never Been Told

'There are songs to sing, there are feelings to feel, there are thoughts to think. That makes three things, and you can't do three things at the same time. The singing is easy, syrup in my mouth, and the thinking comes with the tune, so that leaves only the feelings. Am I right, or am I right?

I can sing the singing, I can think the thinking, but you're not going to catch me feeling the feeling. No, sir.'[173]
Philip Marlowe, in Dennis Potter's *The Singing Detective* (1986)

This was not, as we know, going to be the future. The overwhelming tragedy of what would happen to many of those who worked on *Threepenny* or *Kuhle Wampe* within a few years is inescapable: Ernst Busch would survive the Nazi camps, but some in the supporting cast would not; while Ernst Ottwald and Carola Neher, as refugees in the USSR, would be 'purged' by the end of the decade by the Stalinists, as suspicious foreigners. When these collectives reconstituted themselves after the war, usually in an allegedly 'critical' alliance with Stalinism, there would be a new scepticism and melancholy about the potentialities and conjunctions of the late Weimar era. A haunting song by Brecht and Eisler from 1955, 'The Way the Wind Blows' is a meditation on the sheer disappointment of the apparatuses themselves: 'production and seduction can now be mentioned in the selfsame breath', while the workers are beset by a media which 'tells them what to do and say', and 'are so shy of action' (except of course against Stalinism in East Berlin in 1953), left to 'take their basic pleasures' where they can; while the Communist

Party, the centre of Brecht's most jarring and disjunctive works, from *The Measures Taken* to *Kuhle Wampe*, which should supposedly be able to advocate a way out, is cut off from the workers. But what is advocated here is still essentially the same measure. There's no hermeticism, no retreat, for all the air of weariness: to 'go out where the people go' is the only way out.[174]

If Brecht was sceptical of the efficacy of the Productivist apparatus by the 50s, half a century later we should be even more wary. Soon before he died, Brecht spoke of how 'all that remains of the *Verfremdungseffekten* is the 'effects', stripped of their social application, stripped of their point.'[175] While the theatre might totally disdain 'alienation effects' in favour of realism, you can find something superficially similar all over the 21st century cultural-political landscape: a kind of cynical Brechtian where the alienation effect's insistence of the stepping in and out of roles is a way of avoiding ever actually saying anything, of ever committing: the 'postmodern pathology' of someone like Robbie Williams or Tony Blair resides in their utter inability to step back in after stepping out of Realism.[176] Likewise, watch any video on MTV Base and see a kinetic montage enlisted in the service of slack-jawed ogling. This version of Brechtian technique is never truly dissonant, and of necessity ignores two important components of the Epic Theatre's Apparatus. First, the absence of the democratisation of the apparatuses, and second the absence of the political, educational project.

Yet the first of these two, like the alienation effect, does have a strange presence in current mass culture. What is MySpace if not an utterly degenerated, conformist-individualist version of the *LEF*ists and Tretiakov's Two Way Newspaper? There's no reason to assume that mass access to a means of cultural production automatically results in an interesting product. When everyone is saying nothing we haven't really moved beyond the point where only the elite can say nothing. This is because of the absence of another element of the theoretical apparatus: the Lehre of the

Lehrstück, the insistence on learning and education. The Productive writer for the two way newspaper or the radio of 'exchange' has to become an expert in everything from economics to photography to gesture, and is never allowed to be a mere dilettante. However, these technologies themselves have far more potential than they ever had in 1927. A radio apparatus or a film camera then was essentially ungainly and expensive. Now, a huge quantity of people have some kind of means of cultural production at their fingertips, whether via their cameraphones, cheap DV cameras, blogs, or easily stolen music making programmes like Fruity Loops. That the majority of what is produced by these forms is utterly inane is not necessarily always going to be the case. Capitalism always mistakes its conditions for eternal ones.

Still from Slatan Dudow's Kuhle Wampe

What, then, if all these fragments of the Brechtian apparatus are extant and ineffectual, would it look like if they were used in a manner befitting their democratising, agitational potential? Productivism, in its Soviet and German forms, is now merely a subject for art history, treated with either a reverent enthusiasm or with disdain as technocratic naivete. The fact that the academy is so cut off from the streets that the Productivists considered their natural territory means that nobody seems to have noticed how much the use of new apparatuses advocated by Benjamin or Brecht has been fulfilled in strange and striking ways. Most especially in the dubplate cultures ('scenius' in Brian Eno's phrase) that began in Kingston, Jamaica in the 70s, and percolated into the British 'hardcore continuum', through the common apparatuses of cheap technology and pirate radio. The dubplate was used by Kodwo Eshun in *More Brilliant than the Sun* as a refutation of Benjamin, for its culture of the 'unique copy' – but the culture around it fulfils all the conditions for a Productivist art of the kind Benjamin and Brecht imagined.[177] The future for Productivism, if there is one, will not be on a stage, but coming out of a sound system.

For instance, in the Jamaica of the 1970s there was a means of

Forward! and don't forget wherein lies our strength

Still from Slatan Dudow's Kuhle Wampe

production – cheap 4-track studios, effects pedals and the manipulation of tape – which was both technologically advanced and accessible; and a means of distribution, on the shoddily pressed 7 inch single or dubplate. This technologically disjunctive music is then used as communication, in essentially same way as the

two-way newspaper: as Chuck D pointed out, Hip Hop was for some time the 'Black CNN'.[178] As this was a period of heightened political struggle, this communication frequently had an agitational urgency: Brecht and Eisler would have been very pleased to have written something like Dennis Brown's 'What about the Half'.[179] The historical brutalities – slavery, in this song – that have long been 'kept a big secret' are revealed, history is challenged, the familiar is made strange, and *thought* about what is seemingly self-evident is advocated.

The potential is all still there, in every technologically advanced corner of the world (by now, practically all of it) for the process to be restarted, for the creation of a collectivist, oppositional culture that doesn't shelter in an imagined past, that isn't afraid of proposing its own future. There is always an alternative.

Afterwards

The Unmaking of a Counter-Culture

'That's where money don't matter
In the future
Material things, they don't matter
In the future
I travel in a time machine, I'm in the future'
Wiley, 'Ice Rink' (2003)

So what, you might have the right to ask, is all this *for*? An aesthetic *Ostalgie*, only this time for a past that never even came into existence? An art-historical drift through the past for the edification of those of us lucky enough to be at a safe historical distance?

A possible conclusion, and one that I want to avoid, is that this is all we *can* do now – sift through past battles, past styles, make out of them some sort of composite, fashionable for a fortnight or two. Journey through the picturesque ruins, enjoy the naivete and idealism of the recent past, then return refreshed to a world without politics, a world without what used to be called a counter-culture. Because really, that (tainted as it is by association with the late 1960s to the point where it now evokes a sort of *Easy Rider* flag-and-dick-waving rather than any real attempt at counter-hegemony) is what this book is essentially about. Not the idea that possessing the right clothes and the right books makes you a political initiate, but rather Modernism itself as counter-culture, drawing on sexual politics, industrial aesthetics, critical theory, a new urbanism, in order to suggest – 'as a tradition and as a vision' – the possible outlines of a world after capitalism.

For Jean Baudrillard, writing in 1971 when something called a counter-culture still vaguely existed, such an attempt was misbegotten from the outset. In a piece for the architectural journal *Utopie*, 'Requiem for the Media', he mocked the idea that the mass media have some kind of democratic, socialist teleology inherent in them – a 'potentiality', as Brechtians might put it – which are exactly the terms of these essays. Baudrillard's attack centres on the contention that a reversed media would essentially exist on the same terms as its capitalist competitor. This would automatically neutralise any critical efficacy that it might have, slotting it right back into the spectacle – this is the folly that 'content' can be changed without changing form, already familiar to Marxist Modernists like Hanns Eisler or Karel Teige. Yet even they imagined that mass songs or minimum dwellings could be counter-cultural. On the contrary, a real revolutionary aesthetic strategy would be an immediate, urbanist one, based on a form in which *response*, as opposed to reversal, would break the rules altogether. *Pace* Mayakovsky, the squares should be our palettes, the streets our brushes:

'Walls and words, silk-screen posters, and hand-printed flyers were the true revolutionary media in May (1968), the streets where speech started and was exchanged: everything that is an immediate inscription, given and exchanged, speech and response, moving in the same time and in the same place, reciprocal and antagonistic. The street is in this sense the alternative and subversive form of all the mass media because it is not, like them, an objectified support for messages without response, a distant transit network. It is the cleared space of the symbolic exchange of ephemeral and mortal speech, speech that is not reflected on the Platonic screen of the media. Institutionalised by reproduction, spectacularised by the media, it burst.'[180]

With this comes the truism that the revolution itself doesn't throw up a revolutionary art, and accordingly it is the aesthetics of 1927 rather than 1917 which are central to this book. It's arguable, of course, that the new models – those which produce such overwhelming inanity today – have far more possibility for response than did television or film. But just as xeroxing would be limited by the Xerox company, the terms of our response might be circumscribed by Blogger or Murdoch's MySpace, although whether this applies to, say, Open Access software is a moot point. Baudrillard's dismissal of the possibility of a 'revolutionary' mediation strikes at the heart of any counter-cultural ambitions. Nonetheless, these essays are written in the belief that, while technology is not neutral, it *can* prefigure redemption through reproduction. Meanwhile, the claim that democratising the reproductive technologies, each participant of the Lehrstücke having their own apparatus, inevitably results in banality ('if each of us possessed our own walkie-talkie or Kodak, and made his or her own films, we know what would result: personalised amateurism, the equivalent of Sunday *bricolage* on the periphery of the system'[181]) would suggest that Baudrillard had never listened to London pirate radio.

Towards a New Proletcult

> '*Full of fictitious concern for the calamity that a realised utopia could inflict on mankind, he refuses to take note of the real and far more urgent calamity that prevents the utopia from being realised. It is idle to bemoan what will become of men when hunger and distress have disappeared from the world*'.
> Theodor Adorno, 'Aldous Huxley and Utopia'[182]

This is all very well – but *who* is this for? Left Modernism was intended not just to be tendentious, but to produce effects, to do stuff. Not as a substitute for political action, but as a component of it. This isn't a book of political strategy, and isn't about to offer a solution to the grim state of the British left: but it does try to

121

bring together certain strands, certain ideas which ought to be useful to it should it finally reconstitute or become something new entirely.

To briefly turn to autobiography again, hopefully not as self-indulgence but as illustration, the interest in Modernism exhibited here comes from a few sources. The buildings of the 1960s, dotted around my home town; my Dad's book collection, with its Orwell, Sartre and books on Marxism and working class history; and a teenhood obsessed with the music press, particularly the *Melody Maker*, wherein mass-produced popculture might be discussed and dissected, by the likes of Simon Reynolds, Neil Kulkarni or Taylor Parkes, with the political and theoretical seriousness (if none of the ponderous prose) usually reserved for the novel and the occasional art-house film. I went from there to books by Jon Savage, Greil Marcus, with their recondite historical references and re-imaginings of the familiar past in apocalyptic, revolutionary terms. I would have had a political bent anyway for one reason or another, but these were the reasons why I ended up thinking that a new society ought not to resemble the old.

In *The Road to Wigan Pier* George Orwell claimed, convincingly, that the failure of an idea so self-evidently sensible as Socialism to make real inroads into British society – to put it in terms he would have loathed, to become counter-hegemonic – was at root a failure of propaganda. Socialism was associated with the following two tendencies, which sound rather mutually exclusive. First, the back-to-nature 'prig's paradise' of the garden cities, 'sandal wearers', faddists and ruralists; and second, an H.G Wells-like science fiction machine utopianism, which often tied in with the techno-romanticism of the 'cult of Russia', all those Constructivist photos of glittering tractors and the Dnieper dam. Both of these are considered to be essentially alien to the British worker, and the part of the middle-classes disaffected enough to be won to the cause. The ordinary British proletarian, for Orwell, is essentially conservative, wanting little more out of life than a comfy chair, the

Lydia Thompson, 'Slumber Lions'

kids playing in the corner, the dog lying by the coal fire, the wife sewing and the paper with the racing finals: a 'perfect symmetry…on winter evenings after tea, when the fire glows in the open range', etc. That might still be true, here and there (albeit replacing the hearth with the TV), and it would be silly to object to comfy chairs and familial warmth out of principle. Yet Modernist socialists were, supposedly, bent on wiping all this out. 'Hardly one of the things I have written about will still be there…it is hardly likely that Father will be a rough man with enlarged hands…there won't be a coal fire in the grate, only some kind of invisible heater. The furniture will be made of rubber, glass and steel…And there won't be so many children, either, if the birth-controllers have their way.'[183] Stop for a moment, though, and think of what constituted so much of working class culture, even in 1936: the 'canned' music he despised, resorts like Blackpool with their shiny concrete picture palaces, iron towers and neon lights. An allegedly simple, hidebound and placid people were quite prepared to explore a Modernist environment, if it were dedicated to pleasure rather than worthy edification.

Over 70 years later, if we look at the art forms thrown up by sections of the class Orwell idealised, what are they actually like? Just before writing this I watched a DVD of New Order playing in Brussels in 1981. These three men and one woman, all from working class backgrounds in post-industrial, council-estate Manchester – the grandchildren of those sturdy Wigan men reading the racing pages – were playing music which would have astonished and mortified Orwell, what with its blocks of overwhelming electronic sound, unnatural bass rumbles and technocratic shimmers. A retort might be that all this is just a reflection of the environment, and that in a better world someone like Dizzee Rascal or Ruff Sqwad wouldn't be making sharp, angular, brutal noises via pirated computer programs but whittling sticks or sitting round the fire wassailing. This is a reductio ad absurdum. But if ordinary people are so hostile to new forms, new noises and new shapes, then how did the last forty years of all kinds of jarring, avant-garde street music manage to happen? Were the teds, the mods (Modernists, as they were originally known), glam rockers, punks, junglists, even the kids in provincial towns getting wrecked on Saturday nights to the ludicrously simple and artificial hard house or happy hardcore, all somehow class traitors?

These cultures aren't necessarily revolutionary, or even counter-cultural in the mildest sense. The Baudrillard of 1971 might well have regarded them as a mere distraction, a safety valve, and in many ways they are. Yet isn't it possible to imagine that a new left would want to base a new appeal, a propagandistic force, on these kinds of new desires and forms, rather than on

Eros House, Catford

Hovis advert sentiment, or an interminable wait for the cataclysmic event where all this insurrectionary spontaneity could burst out? All of the art forms written about in this book share one thing – they placed themselves in the everyday, whether in the form of immersive architectural or cinematic space or the reform of Byt itself. All of them tried to step outside of the 'Platonic screen' in its many forms: the place they always wanted to be was *out in the streets.*

What we might just get instead is the appropriation of any aesthetic revolt by the Right, as for instance in much Hip Hop's current role as capitalism's glossily brutal advertising service.[184] The most famous example of this has always been the Italian Futurists, the Fascist Modernists par excellence. Yet even here a little digging in the history of cultural politics reminds us that things could have been different. Antonio Gramsci wrote in 1922 that 'before the war, Futurism was very popular with workers. During the numerous Futurist art events, in the theatres of the largest Italian cities workers took the Futurists' side, and defended them against the attacks of the bourgeois and semi-bourgeois youth, who often came to blows with them.'[185] He went on to suggest that an Italian Proletcult ('Proletarian Culture') movement absorb the best elements of Futurism. The Italian Socialist Party wasn't nearly so keen, and the possibility of a working class futurism disappeared, with the Futurists themselves yoking their work to Fascism.

Futurism would seem a rather peculiar ambition today. If there is one thing about which we can be absolutely certain, it's that the world as we know it is not going to last. As stock markets crash and ice caps melt, the future is something faced with trepidation – perhaps one explanation for Britain's nostalgia. There is always the possibility of another outcome, where this system based on destruction, injustice and barbarism can finally be given its long overdue burial. The dormant Socialist Modernism can, if nothing else, offer spectral blueprints for such a future.

Acknowledgements

Thank you to everyone who read and commented on the manuscript or on earlier versions: Nina Power, Anindya Bhattacharyya, Dominic Fox, Simon Reynolds, John Jourden, Tariq Goddard, R. William Barry, Mark Fisher, Esther Leslie, and especially Roger Gathman and Benjamin Noys.

Thanks to Vladimir Sedach for translation, to Michael Carr for invaluable reproductive assistance, and also to Dušan Makavejev for kindly giving permission to use images from his films.

Belated thanks to Maggie Fricker, both for constant support and for setting a militant example, and to Steve Hatherley and Lorna Maughan for keeping lots of books around. In memoriam: Peter Maughan.

Much appreciation due also to Nikolai Onoufriev and Richard Pare for kind permission to use their photographs, and apologies to Richard for the transfer of his colour photographs to monochrome in this book.

Ta especially to my esteemed comrades Lydia Thompson, Douglas Murphy and Joel Anderson, for giving their time, energy and considerable talents to this project.

London, 2008.

Notes

Forwards

1 *A Book of Ruskin*, edited by E.M Hewetson (Thomas Nelson, 1940), p87-8

2 Walter Benjamin, *Selected Writings, Volume Two, Part Two* (Harvard, 1999), p701-2

3 ibid., p543

4 El Lissitzky, 'A Series of Skyscrapers for Moscow' (1926) in Catherine Cooke, *Russian Avant-Garde Theories of Art, Architecture and the City* (Wiley, 1995), p198

5 Quoted in Reyner Banham, *Theory and Design in the First Machine Age* (Butterworth, 1988), p134-5

6 Martin Pawley, *Terminal Architecture* (Reaktion, 1998), p98 and 214

7 *The Modern Movement in Architecture: Selections from the DOCOMOMO Register*, edited by Catherine Cooke and Dennis Sharp (010, 2000), p7

8 Walter Benjamin, *The Arcades Project* (Harvard, 2002), p473

9 David Lloyd & Nikolaus Pevsner, *The Buildings of England: Hampshire and the Isle of Wight* (Penguin, 1966)

10 A collection of profiles of such fantastical spaces of exclusion and neoliberalism can be found in the Mike Davis and Daniel Bertrand-Monk edited *Evil Paradises* (New Press, 2007), showing a remarkable degeneration of the utopian imaginary, where the ideal world is a kitschified version of the 19th century, the medieval, or frequently, it would seem, 1980s cinema. Utopia is always ready to turn into ideology, and neoliberalism is by no means *always* its antagonist. Indeed, it has its own utopian fictions, as China Mieville's essay in the above collection demonstrates, with its libertarian floating cities. That said, the deficiencies of these tax-free security utopias speak for themselves.

11   Lynsey Hanley, *Estates: An Intimate History* (Granta, 2007)

12   For more on this and more of the like, see the films *The Occupation* and *The London Particular*, at thelondonparticular.org

13   'Within architecture itself, the taste for *dériving* tends to promote all sorts of new forms of labyrinths made possible by modern techniques of construction'. Guy Debord, 'Theory of the *Dérive* ', in *The Situationist International Anthology* (Bureau of Public Secrets, 1995), p53. This was about *creating* environments, via the imagination, the drawing board or the barricade, rather than taking them as they stand.

14   *Estates*, p124

15   Or as it was supposed to be before the Cold War intruded, *Lenin* Court – near Tecton's memorial to Lenin, a local at one time. Allegedly, after incessant vandalism from local Fascists, Lubetkin buried the memorial on site, and it is more than likely rotting away beneath a patch of grass in Kings Cross right now.

16   John Allan, *Lubetkin and the Tradition of Progress* (RIBA, 1992), p366

17   These two founding myths of postmodernism are a little historically dubious; Ronan Point's collapse was due to both the stacking by contractors of a system designed for 6 storeys up to 22, and a tenant getting a non-professional to fix the gas; and the dynamited Pruitt-Igoe estate in St Louis was a failure of an early attempt at desegregation more than it ever was of modern design. It was never replaced.

18   In fact with the latter architects, or the likes of Future Systems, there is the curious phenomenon of something previously considered unbuildable or dreamlike being constructed and seeming merely *boring*, a sort of CGI architecture which resembles a computer generated model even when built.

19   Leon Trotsky, *Literature and Revolution* (Red Words, 1991),

p161-2

Part One

[20] The Fall, *Hex Enduction Hour*, (Kamera, 1982)

[21] See the reviews and features in everything from The *Times* to the *Telegraph*, but typical is Robert Hughes' in The *Guardian* (20/3/2006). Hughes was a pioneer of this pragmatist triumphalism in *The Shock of the New* (Thames & Hudson, 1980), one of the first to make the since commonplace link Modernism=Utopianism=Stalinism or Fascism (take your pick), and to uphold the strict divide between art and life, for which he deserves some sort of credit. Perhaps the strangest and most fascinating response to what was, after all, a surprisingly historically and politically sharp exhibition was by Mark Sinker. An ongoing piece evocatively entitled 'A Dalek made of Light', it winds through Modernism's hygienic impulses, a defence of the re-enactment and the question, very important for our purposes here, of what building for a new society means when the new society fails to materialise. See freakytrigger.co.uk/ft/2006/11/three-point-two-seven-modernist-conundra, freakytrigger.co.uk/ft/2007/02/your-own-private-quatre-bras.

[22] To illuminate this phrase a little, think of the difference between Simon Schama's ingratiating bumbling and A.J.P Taylor's casual respect for his audience's intelligence.

[23] *The Perfect Home* (Channel 4, 2006)

[24] Reyner Banham, *The New Brutalism – Ethic or Aesthetic?* (Architectural Press, 1966), p12. The other serious British modernisms, the Futuristic fantasies of Archigram (some of whose members worked on the South Bank Centre's ferroconcrete walkways by day) and the subsequent high-tech of Foster and Rogers, are outgrowths of Brutalism, not of the International Style. Imagine Rogers' Lloyds building, with its bared services, in concrete rather than steel, and you would

have something very close indeed to Owen Luder and Rodney Gordon's reviled, demolished Tricorn centre in Portsmouth.

25 The relation of Brutalism to the war is complicated, in that it was opposed to the immediate wave of optimistic, socialistic planning that marked out say, Nye Bevan's housing policies, the burst of socialism after the war that created the NHS. If there were 'Bevanite' architects, then they were in Tecton. Bevan laid the first stone at their Spa Green Estate in Finsbury, and Lubetkin's tendency to retire in disgust (at least twice) points to an intractable hatred of Butskellite compromise (see John Allan, *Lubetkin*, p405). The Brutalists meanwhile abhorred, not necessarily the politics, but the ingratiating tendencies of this sort of work, the alleged 'whimsy' of the Festival of Britain, all that patterning and picturesque planning. 'People's Detailing' was the insult of choice.

26 Similarly, Peter Mandler writes in the essay 'New Towns for Old': 'In the plans that emerged after 1945...British modernity was converging upon, not diverging from, Continental experiences. In the course of the 1950s, however, this convergence was aborted. The modernity of the planners, never firmly seated in as anti-bureaucratic and market-driven a polity as Britain's, was dismantled by conservative govern-ments and a different version of modernity was substi-tuted...as a result, across Britain, more historic townscapes were erased, more anonymous commercial architecture was permitted...' etc, in *Moments of Modernity: Reconstructing Britain 1945-64* (Rivers Oram Press, 1999), p208-226. The leftist planners and architects who briefly dominated under Attlee were sidelined after 1951 in favour of developers, yet are still the usual punching bag for the latter's schemes.

27 1949 obituary, quoted in *Edward Wadsworth. Genius of Industrial England* (Arkwright Art Trust, 1990) p16

28 As described by Gillian Darley, the modular construction and large windows used by the architect, one Colonel Greene, were remarkable prefigurings of Modernism, but of necessity hidden as: 'disturbingly bald to the Victorian eye'. Gillian Darley, *Factory* (Reaktion, 2003) 109-11 and Nikolaus Pevsner, *Pioneers of Modern Design from William Morris to Walter Gropius* (Pelican 1974) p124. The definitive work on British industrial 'architecture' is J.M Richards' Dibnah-esque *The Functional Tradition* (Architectural Press, 1958). The aesthetic appeal of the inhuman, put in mild and civilised prose. 'One of the most important effects aesthetically of the industrial revolution was the introduction into the landscape of structures that had nothing to do with the human scale, but reflected rather the superhuman nature of the new industrial activities.' (p20)

29 Karl Marx, *Capital*, volume one: 'To work at a machine, the workman should be taught from childhood, in order that he may learn to adapt his own movements to the uniform and unceasing motion of an automaton...at the same time that factory work exhausts the nervous system to the uttermost, it does away with the many-sided play of the muscles, and confiscates every atom of freedom, both in bodily and intellectual activity...it is not the workman that employs the instruments of labour, but the instruments of labour that employ the workman.' (George Allen & Unwin, 1946, p420-3)

30 Jean-Francois Lyotard, *Libidinal Economy* (Continuum, 2004) p109-10

31 The conflict between the British myth and reality is a Victorian hangover. 'The social and political practices maintain a remarkable, if superficial, continuity with the past...at the same time this is in many respects the country that has broken most radically with all previous ages in human history.' Eric Hobsbawm, *Industry and Empire* (Penguin, 1967), p15. Yet the lack of an authentic 'folk' culture outside of state pageantry is surely one of the principal reasons for Britain's atypical origi-

nality and audacity in pop culture, if practically nowhere else.

32 The head of the Soviet Commissariat of Enlightenment, Anatoly Lunacharsky, worried in 1926: 'certainly mechanised urbanism is one source of images for proletarian poetry, but it cannot serve our needs, since it can only drive the proletariat towards *its own lack of humanity and personality*, and that we absolutely do not want.' My italics. Quoted in Catherine Cooke, *Russian Avant-Garde Theories*, p193

33 Humphrey Jennings, *Pandaemonium* (Picador 1985) p3-5. Jennings also makes the connection between architecture and rationalised, machinic modernity by following *Paradise Lost* with the founding statement of the Royal Society: with Christopher Wren as a founding member.

34 William Blake, *The Marriage of Heaven and Hell* (Oxford, 1975), p6: note also his 'printing-house in Hell'.

35 It's no coincidence that Owenism, the utopian socialist movement that introduced the term into British political life, was centred on a specific factory, Robert Owen's New Lanark. Equally as important, of course, are the proletarian machine-wreckers of the same period. On Owen, Robert Southey, visiting New Lanark in 1819 and rehearsing many sceptical anti-utopians that would follow him: '(Owen) makes these *human machines*, as he calls them (and he literally believes them to be) as happy as he can, and makes a display of their happiness. And he jumps to the monstrous conclusion that because he can do this with 2210 persons who are totally dependent upon him – all mankind can be governed with the same facility. *Et in Utopia ego*. But I never regarded man as a machine...could not suppose, as Owen does, that men may be cast in a mould (like the other parts of his mill) and take the impression with certainty...He keeps out of sight from himself, and others, that his system, instead of aiming at perfect freedom, can only be kept in power by absolute

power.' 'Journal of a Tour in Scotland in 1819', in Jennings, *Pandaemonium*, p157-8. See also Hobsbawm, *Industry and Empire*, p66-7.

36 Charles Dickens, *Hard Times* (Penguin, 1994), p1

37 Evgeny Zamyatin, *The Islanders* (Trilogy, 1978) p7

38 Wyndham Lewis (ed), *BLAST* (Black Sparrow Press, 1981), p51-85

39 Paul Overy, 'Vorticism' in, *Concepts of Modern Art from Fauvism to Postmodernism* (Thames & Hudson 1993) p109

40 As such, it was totally opposed to the late 19th century's Romantic Socialism, whether Morris, the Garden Cities (given a specific Blasting by C.R.W Nevinson) or Arts & Crafts, all explicitly anti-machine. On the these exemplars of a non-Brutalist British socialist aesthetic, which are not given their due in the present work, see

themeasurestaken.blogspot.com/2007/04/revolution-in-garden.html

41 Wyndham Lewis, *Blasting and Bombardiering* (London, 1937), p35

42 See also C.R.W Nevinson's 'Loading timber at Southampton Dock'. Nevinson, though an 'English Futurist' rather than an official Vorticist, chose the title *BLAST*. This painting depicts the proletariat as the inorganic collectivity, fusing with the red timbers. This should not be regarded as some sort of intentionally socialist aesthetic, however. Wadsworth was a factory-owner's son, and gave his services and his car to the government in the general strike of 1926.

43 *BLAST*, p33

44 Wyndham Lewis, *The Caliph's Design – Architects, where is your Vortex?* (The Egoist, 1919) p29

45 Wyndham Lewis, 'Plain House-Builder, Where is Your Vorticist?' in *Creatures of Habit and Creatures of Change* (Black Sparrow Press, 1989) p245-56. Perhaps steps in this direction were made by Wells Coates, a disciple of Lewis' – the Isokon

building in London, with its masses of sculpted concrete was intriguingly described as 'protobrutalist' by Manfredo Tafuri and Francesco Dal Co, in *Modern Architecture* (Faber 1986), p230

46 Anthony Burgess, *A Clockwork Orange* (Penguin, 1972) p27

47 Martin Pawley wrote in *Terminal Architecture* that war, (which might entail extreme precision in engineering) was central to the experience of brutalist-associated architects like James Stirling, and 'no able-bodied architect of the modern era of military age who did not see service in either world war could ever be wholly admired' (p141-2). It's arguable that one of the stylistic antecedents of the New Brutalism (at least in its late 60s versions, when it became a mannerism of the rough and oblique) was the military architecture necessitated by the fear of German invasion. The Pillboxes and bunkers of 1940, with their raw concrete and angular inscrutability, were more akin to the average Brutalist structure than was much classical Modernism.

48 The Smithsons have remained popular in universities, seemingly more for their theorising than their practice: unsurprisingly perhaps, given how few commissions they received, but nonetheless an evasion of the concrete presence of their work.

49 Reyner Banham, 'The New Brutalism', *Architectural Review* 118, 1955, in *A Critic Writes* (University of California, 1996), p9

50 Alison and Peter Smithson, 'House of the Future at the Ideal Home Exhibition', 1956, in *The Charged Void: Architecture* (Monacelli Press 2001), p176

51 Team X, the group that killed the CIAM, and with it 'classical' Modernism, coalesced around this project.

52 Constant Nieuwenhuis, New Babylon's designer along with Debord, would have been aware of the Smithsons' work via his contacts in the Dutch wing of Team X.

53 Alison and Peter Smithson, 'Criteria for Mass Housing',

1957/9
54 Alison and Peter Smithson, 'Robin Hood Gardens', in *The Charged Void*, p296-7

55 Since this was first written, *Building Design* set up a petition to 'save' Robin Hood Gardens, garnering the support of the cream of the architects of the last two decades, almost all of whom have never had the opportunity to design social housing. Whether this will sway Tower Hamlets council from their determination to serve the local plutocrats is unknown at the time of going to press.

56 *Thamesmead* (Greater London Council, 1967)

57 In the late 60s and 70s, when continental or American directors wanted the future built and pre-prepared, they went to Britain. Kubrick with Thamesmead (his first British film), but also Truffaut's use of the LCC's Brutalist flagship, the towers of Alton West, in *Fahrenheit 451*, or Antonioni's exploration of Patrick Hodgkinson/Camden Council's Brunswick Centre in *The Passenger*.

58 *Thamesmead Project 05*, at http://homepage.ntlworld.com/rachel.barbaresi/mainhtml/work05.htm#

59 Catherine Croft, *Concrete Architecture* (Gibbs Smith, 2006), p8

60 Banham, *A Critic Writes*, p31

61 Pulp, 'Sheffield: Sex City', on *Intro* (Island, 1993)

62 This film is available for viewing at the BFI's Mediatheque, London.

63 Mark Owens, 'New Brutalists/New Romantics', in Zak Kyes & Mark Owens (eds), *Forms of Inquiry – The Architecture of Critical Graphic Design* (AA, 2007)

64 At their Party conference – the prospective demolisher was the young William Hague. Lyric from The Human League, 'Blind Youth' on *Reproduction* (Virgin, 1979)

65 Japan, 'Halloween' on *Quiet Life* (Ariola, 1979), Ultravox, 'My Sex' on *Ultravox!* (Island, 1977)

66   The 'hardcore continuum' is expounded at greatest length in
     Energy Flash (Picador 1998). Also relevant here is the apposite
     claim that grime is a direct reflection of London's built
     aesthetics in 'Against All Odds', a piece on grime included in
     Bring the Noise (Faber, 2007)
67   By which I am in no way referring to the gallery-bound
     games and third-hand poses of the 90s' 'Young British Art'.
68   Blomfield, *Modernismus* (Macmillan, 1934), p164.The instincts
     I'm implying here aren't really those invoked by the book's
     author. This famously blimpish critique of 'aesthetic
     Bolshevism' by the architect of Regent Street and Goldsmiths
     College is well worth reading, if only to see how close his
     arguments are to those of, say, Simon Jenkins or Leon Krier,
     though both are savvy enough to avoid rhetoric like 'the new
     architecture is deliberately cosmopolitan. For myself, I am
     prejudiced enough to detest cosmopolitanism. I am for the
     hill on which I was born. France for the French, Germany for
     the Germans, England for the Englishman' (p82)
69   *Kidbrooke Vision*, Greenwich Borough Council (2002)
     'Traditional streets are the defining elements of the proposal.
     There is an emphasis on natural surveillance provided by
     situating dwellings along street and small parks to form a
     well-defined public realm. There is no confusion about what
     is public and what is private...', p16. Not all of the surveil-
     lance will be natural, of course.
70   This doesn't imply that council tenants like rotting buildings,
     pissed-in lifts and meagre facilities, just that such things are
     contingent and not architectural. Although in the case of
     Kidbrooke, opposition might have more than a little to do
     with the pittance residents who bought their flats have been
     offered to sell up by the local council – as little as one sixth of
     their likely market value. See
     http://www.bbc.co.uk/london/content/articles/2006/12/21/
     kidbrooke_feature.shtml, and the Defend Council Housing

campaign at http://www.defendcouncilhousing.org.uk/dch/.

Part Two

71 Arkady & Boris Strugatsky, *Roadside Picnic* (Millennium, 2007), P36

72 *Red Planet Mars,* directed by Harry Horner, 1952, only the tip of an iceberg of occasionally glorious McCarthyite trash.

73 On the Posadists, believers in permanent interstellar revolution, see Matt Salusbury's two pieces in the *Fortean Times*, August 2003.

74 Viktor Shklovsky, *Knight's Move* (Dalkley, 2005) p21-4

75 The nearest equivalents are the discussion of early Soviet SF in Darko Suvin's *Metamorphoses of Science Fiction* (New Haven, 1979), and Richard Stites' *Revolutionary Dreams: Utopian vision and Experimental Life in the Russian Revolution* (Oxford, 1989). A passage from the latter inadvertently describes the conjuncture of the present work. 'Soviet science fiction lies before us like archaeological rubble…popular culture of a bygone age, taking its place in the mausoleum of visions and fantasies and perceptions, along with American comic strips, pulp magazines and war cards of the 1920s and 30s, a rich tapestry of crude colour and cartoon figures', p189.

76 Vladimir Papernyi's 1979 distinction between the light, fast, weightless 'culture one' of the Constructivists and the drab, earthbound 'culture two' of Stalin, Khrushchev and Brezhnev is instructive here. See Susan Buck-Morss, *Dreamworld and Catastrophe* (MIT, 2002), p121-22

77 Bertolt Brecht, *Poems Part Two* (Methuen, 1976), p192

78 T.J Clark, *Farewell to an Idea* (Yale University Press, 1999), p1-7

79 Richard Pare, *The Lost Vanguard* (Monacelli Press, 2007), p222-7

80 Pare, p230-3

81 These elements were described as a 'component fixation' in Kestutis Paul Zygas' study *Form Follows Form: the Source*

Imagery of Constructivist Architecture (Ann Arbor, 1981)

82 That is, in Sigfried Giedion's historicising *Building in France, Building in Iron, Building in Ferroconcrete* (G, 1995) which claims the great 19th century engineers as 'Constructivists', and Karel Teige's *The Minimum Dwelling* (MIT, 2002), a polemical, engaged argument for Constructivist housing.

83 Philip Johnson & Henry-Russell Hitchcock, *The International Style* (Norton 1966), p93

84 J.M Richards, *Modern Architecture* (Pelican, 1953), p85. This book also contains a largely accurate diagnosis of the failure of Soviet modernism as the product of poor technologies and the requirements of an authoritarian government with a largely rural population. But bizarrely, in the first edition of the book (1940), Richards listed Moisei Ginsburg, Tatlin and El Lissitsky, at least one of whom had actually got his designs built. Their replacement seems purely a product of cold war imperatives.

85 Usually ignoring the fine work in English on the subject: translations of Anatole Kopp's *Town and Revolution* (Thames & Hudson, 1970) and Selim Khan-Magomedov's *Pioneers of Soviet Architecture* (Thames & Hudson, 1988) and the brilliant publications and translations of the late Catherine Cooke in *AD* and elsewhere.

86 Aleksandr Rodchenko, *Experiments for the Future* (MOMA, 2005) p304-8

87 *Moscow Heritage at Crisis Point*, eds Clementine Cecil & Edward Harris (MAPS 2007), p105

88 This isn't necessarily the architects' own fault. On Hadid, see 'When the Art of Building is Commanded by Capital', *Socialist Worker*, 21st July 2007

89 Leon Trotsky, 'From the Old Family to the New' in *Problems of Everyday Life* (Monad, 1973), p42

90 In the divide between revolutionary legislation and revolutionary praxis – concentration on the former being socialist

Byt's downfall, according to Wilhelm Reich's *The Sexual Revolution* (Vision, 1972) – the social condenser is clearly on the side of the latter.

[91] See Victor Buchli's *An Archaeology of Socialism* (Berg, 2000)

[92] *Moscow Heritage at Crisis Point* p44-9

[93] Buchli, p52

[94] Trotsky, 'Leninism and Workers' Clubs', *Problems of Everyday Life* p288-319

[95] Konstantin Melnikov, 'The Rusakov Workers' Club', in *Architecture of Konstantin Melnikov 1920s-30s*, ed Rishat Mullagildin (Gallery-MA, 2002), P48

[96] El Lissitzky, *Russia: An Architecture for World Revolution* (Lund Humphries, 1970), p44

[97] The British Modernism of the '30s had its own adaptations of these social condensers, occasionally: sometimes directly, in the work of the Soviet émigré Bertold Lubetkin, or more whimsically in Wells Coates' Lawn Road 'Isobar'.

[98] St Petersburg collective Chto Delat/What is to be Done's Narvskaya Zastava 'drift' is a fascinating quasi-Situationist traversal of this district. It can be found online, in English, at http://www.chtodelat.org/images/pdfs/Chtodelat_07.pdf

[99] Nikolai Miliutin, *Sotsgorod* (MIT, 1974), p62

[100] Two choice examples: the architectural illustrations in Anna Louise Strong's *From Stalingrad to the Kuzbas* (Modern Books, 1932), and in J.G Crowther's *Soviet Science* (Pelican, 1936)

[101] For the Izvestia and Mosselprom posters, along with many other popular architectural fantasies of the decade, see Mikhail Anikst & Elena Chernevich, *Soviet Commercial Design of the Twenties* (Thames & Hudson, 1989). The USSR's postwar skyscrapers were another version of New York – but that of the 1910s and the gothic-wedding cake Woolworth building, risibly obscurantist in the decade of the Seagram building and the Unité d'Habitation. On the Stenbergs, see *Stenberg Brothers: Constructing a Revolution in Soviet Design* (MOMA,

1997). Curiously, another example of Modernism-as-propaganda used former Vkhutemas student Berthold Lubetkin's Finsbury Health Centre in London. It rises out of the slums in a WWII poster by Abram Games, with the legend 'YOUR BRITAIN – FIGHT FOR IT NOW'. Apparently, the poster was personally vetoed by Winston Churchill. See Allan, *Lubetkin*, p374-5.

102 Le Corbusier and Nikolai Kolli's Centrosoyus office block in Moscow was referred to by the Stalinised Architects' Union as an 'alien building' on its completion in 1936. Jean-Louis Cohen, *Le Corbusier* (Taschen, 2004, p45)

103 J Hoberman, *The Red Atlantis* (Temple University Press, p145-8): 'what previous political movement had ever devoted itself to liberation of the entire globe? And now: 'follow our example, comrades! Unite into a family of workers in a Martian Union of Soviet Socialist Republics!''

104 According to Pare himself, it is still extremely difficult to get access to these 'New Industrial Cities'.

105 Melnikov, 'The Green City', *Architecture of Konstantin Melnikov 1920s-30s*, p62-69

106 Profiled in Chris Marker's films *The Last Bolshevik* (1992) and *The Train Rolls On* (1970)

107 As the Anarchist army he led in the Russian Civil War apparently described itself. Stites, *Revolutionary Dreams*, p55

108 Mikhail Okhitovich, quoted in S. Frederick Starr, 'Visionary Town Planning', in the collection *Cultural Revolution in Russia, 1928-31* (Midland, 1984) p216

109 A phrase used in Christina Lodder's *Russian Constructivism* (Yale University Press, 1983) to describe the gentle marriages of man, machine and nature in Tatlin and Matyushin. Similar ideas run through Susan Buck-Morss' *Dreamworld and Catastrophe*: the possibility of a redemptive socialist technology rather than the rapacious, environmentally wasteful one that the USSR borrowed from the USA.

[110] Alexander Pasternak was the brother of the Nobel Prize winner Boris, himself very briefly a Constructivist associate of *LEF*. Quoted in Kopp, p177

[111] There's a photograph of a prototype in Khan-Magomedov's *Pioneers of Soviet Architecture*, p387

[112] Moisei Ginzburg to Le Corbusier, quoted in *Town and Revolution*, p252-4

[113] Le Corbusier, *The Radiant City* (Faber, 1967)

[114] Mikhail Okhitovich, quoted in S. Frederick Starr, 'Visionary Town Planning', p215

[115] Superficially, Foster's new Wembley stadium has a distinctly similar silhouette.

[116] Quoted in Hugh D Hudson, 'Terror in Soviet Architecture: the Murder of Mikhail Okhitovich', *Slavic Review*, 1992

[117] Sigfried Giedion, quoted in Eric Mumford, *The CIAM Discourse on Urbanism* (MIT, 2000), p87-88

[118] *Architectural Fantasies*, quoted in *Iakov Chernikhov and Russian Constructivism*, edited by Catherine Cooke (AD 1989), p62

Part Three

[119] Herbert Marcuse, *Negations* (Penguin, 1972) p116

[120] Kate Bush, *Hounds of Love* (EMI, 1986)

[121] JG Ballard, 'A Handful of Dust', *Guardian*, 20th March 2006

[122] Marcuse, p132

[123] 'Many thanks for the gorgeous asters and for Ricarda Huch. Of course, I diligently read the poems at once, but I must confess: female eroticism in public has always been embarrassing to me. As our Auer once said 'One doesn't say things like that, one does them.'' Letter to Mathilde Jacob, 10/11/1915, in *The Letters of Rosa Luxemburg* (edited by Stephen Eric Bronner, Humanities Press 1993, p165)

[124] Wilhelm Reich, *Dialectical Materialism and Psychoanalysis* (Socialist Reproduction, 1972), p45-6

[125] Charles Jencks, *Le Corbusier and the Tragic View of Architecture*

(Penguin, 1987), p104

[126] Jean Louis-Cohen, *Le Corbusier and the Mystique of the USSR* (Princeton University Press, 1992), p116-7

[127] Leonid Sabsovich, *The USSR In Fifteen Years*, quoted in *Town and Revolution* p171-2

[128] Wilhelm Reich, *The Invasion of Compulsory Sex-Morality* (Pelican, 1975), p23-4

[129] ibid, p24

[130] JG Ballard, *The Atrocity Exhibition* (Flamingo, 2001) p86

[131] Sexual banality 'produces the kind of mentality that is not only inimical to the growth of a fully human, living culture, but is in fact its nemesis.' Teige, *The Minimum Dwelling*, p170.

[132] Andrea Dworkin, *Intercourse* (Free Press, 1997), p141

[133] Unpublished, delivered at the Ballard conference 'From Shanghai to Shepperton' at the University of East Anglia, 2007

[134] Marcuse, p116

[135] Iakov Tugedkhol'd, quoted in Christina Kiaer, *Imagine No Possessions* (MIT, 2005), p106

[136] Kiaer, p123

[137] *Mayakovsky and his Poetry*, ed Herbert Marshall (Pilot, 1944) p135

[138] The record in question was Comet Gain's *Say yes! To International Socialism* (Wiiija, 1996)

[139] Vladimir Mayakovsky, *The Bedbug* (Davis-Poynter, 1974), p14

[140] ibid, p10

[141] ibid, p38

[142] ibid, p42

[143] Sergei Tretiakov, quoted in Kiaer, p253

[144] George Orwell, *Nineteen Eighty-Four* (Penguin, 1990), p70

[145] Gang of Four, *Entertainment!* (EMI 1979)

[146] Public Enemy, 'Caught, can I get a Witness?' on *It Takes a Nation of Millions to Hold us Back* (Def Jam, 1988)

[147] Alexandra Kollontai, *Love of Worker Bees* (Virago, 1988), p206-7

[148] Shulamith Firestone's *Dialectic of Sex* (Paladin, 1970) provides a similar argument on the failure of Soviet sexual utopianism, drawing heavily on Reich. Firestone's harsh sexual-technological futurism is a fascinating example of the side of feminism that both sides of the current debate find embarrassing – and in that, is quintessential Sexpol.

[149] Michel Foucault, *History of Sexuality – Introduction* (Penguin, 1990), p5

[150] Another thing for which Sjöman could be blamed/credited is what we could call 'director's Brechtian' – the self-debunking yet frequently tiresome baring of the film director himself. This isn't always a whimsical device though, as anyone who has seen Lindsay Anderson's *O Lucky Man!* (1973) could attest.

[151] Alexander Bogdanov, *Red Star* (Indiana, 1984), p93

[152] Raymond Durgnat, *WR: Mysteries of the Organism* (BFI, 1999), p73

[153] ibid, p47

[154] In *Modernism: An Anthology of Sources and Documents* (EUP, 1999)

Part Four

[155] Bertolt Brecht, *Stories of Mr Keuner* (City Lights, 2001), p64-5

[156] In many ways, the two writers suffer a similar fate, both being neutered by the anti-theory contingent. Channel 4's *Beckett on Film* season, with its contributions from the likes of Damien Hirst, was equally determined to ignore the playwright's strict rules for décor and performance. Nonetheless, Beckett is not so widely considered oppressive and forbidding, perhaps because he kept his own leftism more quiet.

[157] T.W Adorno, 'Commitment' in *Aesthetics and Politics* (Verso 2007)

[158] From Walter Benjamin, 'Conversations with Brecht', in *Aesthetics and Politics*, p97

[159] Walter Benjamin, 'Theatre and Radio – the Mutual Control of

their Educational Programme' in *Selected Writings Volume 2 Part 2* (Harvard 1999) p583-6

160 ibid 768-83

161 'The newspaper can exist because of its collectivist nature...we believe that collectivising the labour of the book is a progressive process...specialists from non-literary fields who have valuable material at their disposal (travel, research, biography, adventure, organisational and scientific experience) enter into the production collective.' Sergei Tretiakov, 'To be Continued' (1929) in *October* 118: Soviet Factography Special Issue, Fall 2006, p53

162 Bertolt Brecht, *On Film and Radio* (Methuen, 2000), p41-9

163 ibid, p35-6

164 ibid, p10

165 Hanns Eisler, 'Misuc', in *Brecht as they Knew Him* edited by Herbert Witt (Lawrence & Wishart, 1980) p94-5

166 Note that both were in periods of intense political struggle.

167 Brecht, *On Film and Radio*, p10-19

168 *Brecht as They Knew Him*, p69-80

169 *On Film and Radio*, p147-202

170 ibid, p207-9

171 Hanns Eisler, *A Rebel in Music* (Kahn and Averill, 1999), p67

172 'On Revolutionary Music' (1932): 'Comprehensibility is to be found solely in the field of popular song, and unfortunately, the mistake is often made of settling for a so-called 'red' popular song. Yet the bourgeois song hit has a corrupt musical passivity which we cannot adopt. The melodic line and the harmony of the popular song are of no use. But it is possible to remould the rhythm of jazz to make it taut and rigorous.' *A Rebel in Music*, p68

173 Dennis Potter, *The Singing Detective* (BBC, 1986)

174 The version referred to here appears on *Robyn Archer Sings Brecht Volume Two* (EMI 1980)

175 John Willett, *The Theatre of Bertolt Brecht* (Methuen, 1977),

p186

[176] See K-Punk, http://k-punk.abstractdynamics.org/archives/009125.html, and for Mark's response to the first version of this piece, go to http://k-punk.abstractdynamics.org/archives/009043.html.

[177] Kodwo Eshun, *More Brilliant than the Sun* (Quartet, 1998), p187-8. Even conceding his point, the fact that the 'unique' technically reproducible dubplate can be taped off the (pirate) radio puts a dent in the remystification.

[178] It's no coincidence that perhaps the most terrifyingly powerful English version of Brecht on record is Nina Simone's version of 'Pirate Jenny', relocating its class war to a 'crummy Southern town'.

[179] Dennis Brown, 'What About The Half' (Trojan, 1974)

Afterwards

[180] Jean Baudrillard, *Utopia Deferred – Writings for Utopie, 1967-1978* (Semiotext(e) 2006), p84

[181] Baudrillard, p91

[182] T.W Adorno, *Prisms* (MIT, 1995), p116-7

[183] George Orwell, *The Road to Wigan Pier* (Penguin, 1988), p104-5

[184] The brilliant blogger Robin Carmody (robincarmody.livejournal.com) wrote persuasively in 2002-3 of a post 9/11 strain of 'Fascist-Hop', a funkless, militaristic form of martial exhortations and marching beats, as heard in tracks like Bonecrusher's 'Never Scared': now seemingly vanished, but a brief and unnerving glimpse of what such a thing might be.

[185] Antonio Gramsci, 'A Letter to Leon Trotsky on Futurism', *Revolutionary History*, Volume 7, No 2, p118-120

Contemporary culture has eliminated both the concept of the public and the figure of the intellectual. Former public spaces – both physical and cultural – are now either derelict or colonized by advertising. A cretinous anti-intellectualism presides, cheerled by expensively educated hacks in the pay of multinational corporations who reassure their bored readers that there is no need to rouse themselves from their interpassive stupor. The informal censorship internalized and propagated by the cultural workers of late capitalism generates a banal conformity that the propaganda chiefs of Stalinism could only ever have dreamt of imposing. Zero Books knows that another kind of discourse – intellectual without being academic, popular without being populist – is not only possible: it is already flourishing, in the regions beyond the striplit malls of so-called mass media and the neurotically bureaucratic halls of the academy. Zero is committed to the idea of publishing as a making public of the intellectual. It is convinced that in the unthinking, blandly consensual culture in which we live, critical and engaged theoretical reflection is more important than ever before.

9781846941764.